STUDY OF THE CELL

For NEET, other competition, and Foundation Classes

Features of this book

- No more long and boring paragraphs!
- Every minute detail from NCERT and Relevant NEET Content is covered.
- Huge collection of MCQ from previous NEET and Other competition exams.

Tauqeer Ahmad

CONTENTS

CELL : THE UNIT OF LIFE

1. DISCOVERY OF CELL

- English physicist **Robert Hooke** in **1665**, while observing cork (bark of a tree) through his microscope (crude microscope).
- He saw **tiny honeycomb**-like structures which were actually dead tissues of an oak tree.
- Robert Hooke saw small compartments as structures, so he coined the term **'Cell'** from the Latin word **'cellula'** which means **'small or tiny compartment' or "little rooms."**
- Robert Hooke makes his own microscope named **crude microscope.**
- Robert Hooke is considered **the father of cytology.**
- Robert Hooke wrote about all these things in his book **Micrographia.**

- In 1676, the first living cell was discovered & described by **Anton van Leeuwenhoek** in pond water.
- Anton van Leeuwenhoek discovered **bacteria** and called them '**animalcules**.'
- Anton van Leeuwenhoek after the discovery of bacteria is known as the **father of bacteria**.
- Anton van Leeuwenhoek invented the first microscope he is known as **the father of microscopy**.
- He is also known for the discoveries of RBC, sperm, and protozoa.
- The first representation of bacteria is to be found in a drawing by Leeuwenhoek in that publication in 1683.

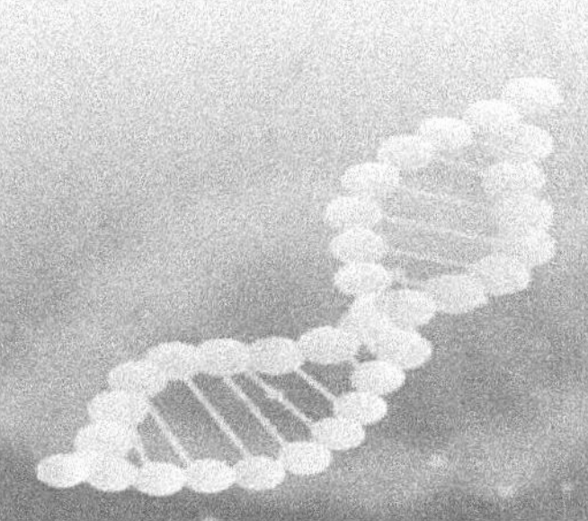

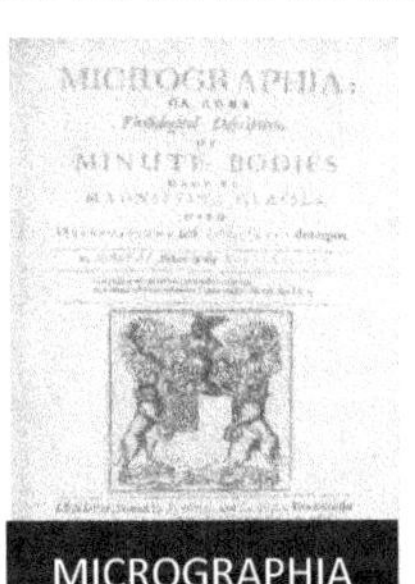

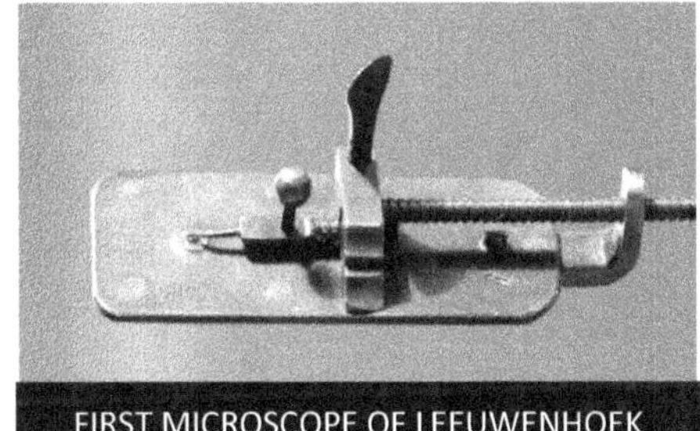

Figure 1: Scientists related Cell discovery

2. CELL THEORY

- The cell theory was formulated by German Botanist Matthias Schleiden in 1838 and British Zoologist Theodor Schwann in 1839.
- After examining a large number of plants, Schleiden observed that all plants are composed of different kinds of cells which form tissues.
- Same time, Schwann studied different types of animals and reported that cells have a thin layer (now known as the plasma membrane).
- Cell theory formulated that
  (i) All living organisms are composed of cells and their products.
  (ii) Cells are structural and functional units of life.

- The cell theory did not explain how new cells were formed.
- In 1855, Rudolf Virchow first explained that new cells are derived from pre-existing cells by cell division *(Omnis cellula-e-cellula)*.
- The previous cell theory was therefore modified into a final one.
- The fundamental features of cell theory are as follows:
  (i) All living organisms are composed of cells and their products.
  (ii) Cells are the structural and functional units of life.
  (iii) All cells arise from pre-existing cells.

Figure 2: Scientists related Cell Theory

Do You Know

➢ Robert Hooke discovered dead cell.
➢ Leeuwenhoek discovered the first living cell.

Definition

➢ The cell is the smallest, basic structural, and functional unit of life.

3. CELL SHAPE & SIZE

- Cells have different shapes and sizes based on organisms and their function.
- Smallest known cell (Length: 0.3 µm) – Mycoplasma or PPLO (Pleuro-Pneumonia Like Organism).
- Largest isolated single cell (Diameter-6 inches with shell) Egg of Ostrich).
- Longest plant cell-Schlerenchymatous fiber.
- Longest animal cell-Neuron.
- Bacteria 3-5 µm.
- Human Red Blood cells 7 µm.
- Cells have variable shapes like (disc), polygonal, columnar, cuboid, spherical, spindle-shaped, irregular, thread-like, etc.
- Shape of cells is related to its function *e.g.*, RBCs are biconcave which helps them to peas through the surface of capillaries.

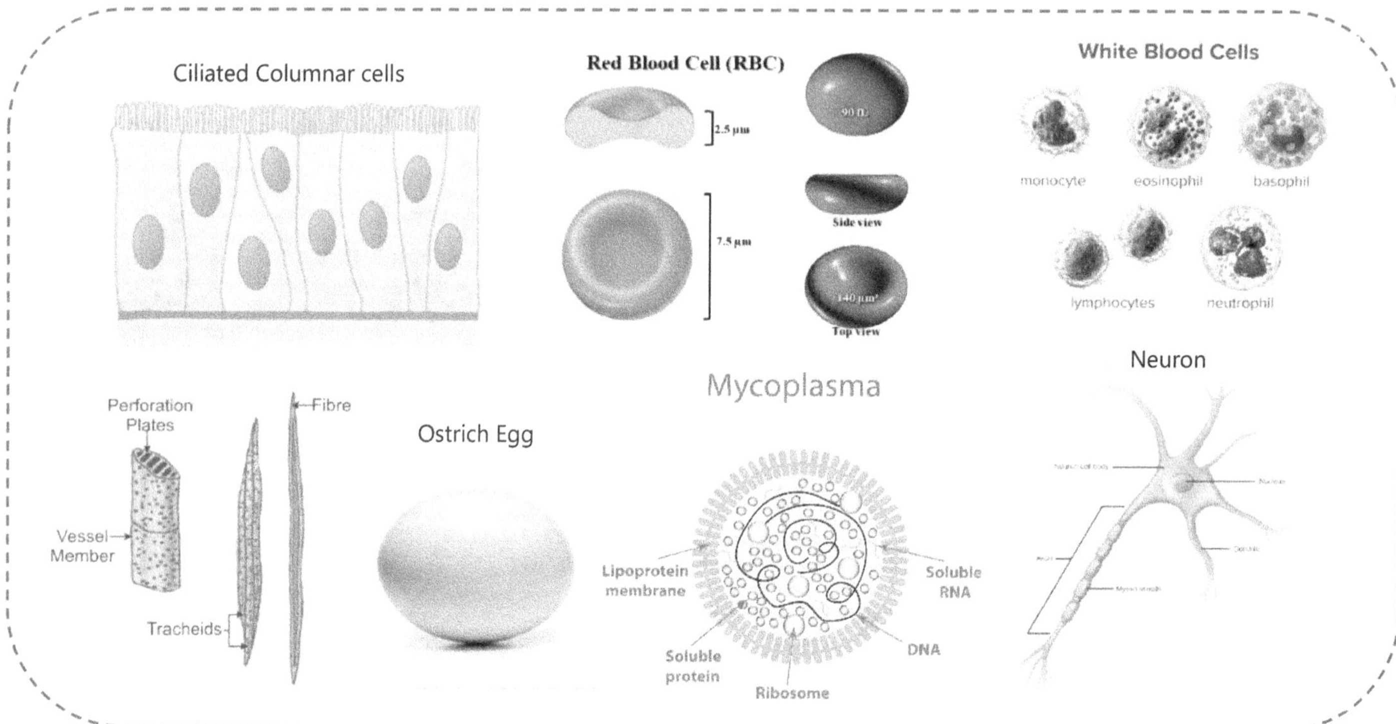

Figure 3: Different shapes of cells

4. PROTOPLASM

- The term protoplasm was coined by J. E. Purkinje in 1835.
- Protoplasm refers to the entire living part of the cell.
- The protoplasm consists of cytoplasm and nucleus. It doesn't contain the cell wall.
- The protoplasm forms 95% of the total weight of a cell.

- Cytoplasm is a thick solution that fills each cell and is enclosed by the cell membrane.
- Cytoplasm refers to the jelly-like part inside the cell excluding the nucleus.
- It is made up of 80% water. It is clear and colorless.
- In prokaryotes, all the cellular contents lie within the cytoplasm because of the lack of a nucleus.
- In eukaryotes, the cytoplasm is encoded within the plasma membrane on one side and nuclear membrane on the other side and consists of cell organelles embedded in it.

Do You Know 

Ectoplasm and Endoplasm
> The cytoplasm of Prokaryotes. *E.g.,* **Amoeba** shows two distinct areas called endoplasm and ectoplasm. The outer membrane below the plasma membrane is known as ectoplasm while the inner dense and granular layer is known as endoplasm.

6. TYPES OF CELLS

❖ All living cells are broadly classified into two types:

```
                            Cells
           ┌──────────────────┴──────────────────┐
   Prokaryotic cell                        Eukaryotic cell
(Pro-primitive, karyon-nucleus)        (Eu-true, karyon-nucleus)
These cells have the primitive         These cells have well defined
type of nucleus called nucleoid        double membrane-bound nucleus.
or genophore.                          All types of cell organelles are found.
No any membranous cell organelle       Example: Protista, fungi, plants, and
found.                                 animals.
They do not have a nuclear membrane.
Example: Bacteria, Mycoplasma, Blue-green
```

Figure 4: Types of cells

7. PROKARYOTIC CELLS

- Prokaryotic cells are smaller than eukaryotic cells.
- They multiply more rapidly.
- They show variation in shape and size.
- The four basic shapes of bacteria are:
- Bacillus: Rod shaped
- Coccus: Spherical shaped
- Vibrio: Comma shaped
- Spirillum: Spiral

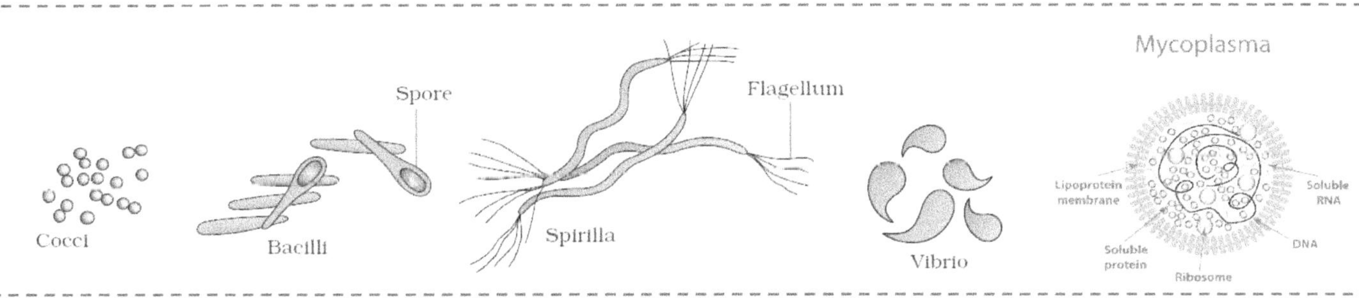

Figure 5: Types of prokaryotic cells

Table 1: Organization of all Prokaryotic cells

Parts	Description
Cell Wall	▪ Present in all prokaryotes except mycoplasma.
Cell Membrane	▪ Present in all prokaryotic cells.
Nucleus	▪ The well-defined nucleus is absent. ▪ Genetic material is naked and dissolves in the cytoplasm (lack of nuclear membrane). ▪ Genetic material is present as circular, double-stranded DNA. ▪ Genetic material is referred to as genophore.
Cytoplasm	▪ Fluid matrix which fills the cells.
Plasmids	▪ Small circular DNA is present outside the genomic DNA present in most bacteria. ▪ Responsible for conferring certain unique phenotypic characteristics. ▪ e.g., antibiotic resistance
Cell organelles	▪ Membrane-bounded cell organelles are absent in all prokaryotes. ▪ Only 70s Ribosome is present (membrane-less cell organelle).
Inclusion body	▪ Unique feature of prokaryotic cells.
Mesosome	▪ Characteristic feature of prokaryotes. ▪ Differentiated form of the cell membrane. ▪ Present as an infolding of the cell membrane. ▪ Contains enzymes associated with respiration and therefore often compared with eukaryotic mitochondria.

7.1 Cell Envelope & its modifications

- Most prokaryotic cells especially bacteria have a chemically complex cell envelope.
- The cell envelope is a tightly bound three-layered structure found in prokaryotes.
- While each layer has a distinct function, all three layers provide a protective covering to the bacteria cell as a single unit.
- The three layers are:
  - Outermost glycocalyx
  - Middle cell wall
  - Inner plasma membrane
- Bacteria can be grouped into two categories on the basis of the cell envelope.
- Due to this difference, they differ in the way they respond to the staining procedure developed by Gram known as **Gram staining.**
- The two categories are:
- **Gram-positive bacteria:** They have a thick cell wall containing many layers of peptidoglycan and teichoic acid. These bacteria are stained violet by primary stain

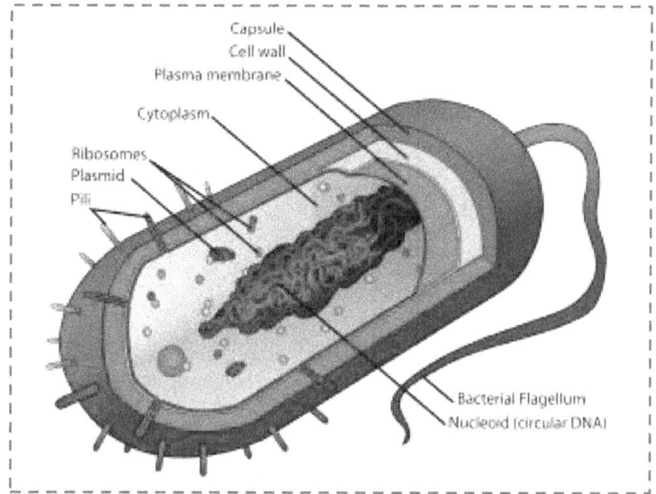

Figure 6: Bacterial cell showing cell envelope

crystal violet during the Gram staining process e.g., *S. aureus.*

- **Gram-Negative bacteria:** They have a thin cell wall with only a few layers of peptidoglycan surrounded by another lipid membrane containing lipoprosachharides and lipoproteins. These bacteria are stained pink by the counterstain safranine during the Gram staining process e.g., *E. coli* and many other pathogenic bacteria.

Table 2: Layers of the cell envelope

Layers	Description
Glycocalyx	▪ Composition and thickness differ among different bacteria. ▪ Can be present as a loose sheath called slime layer in some bacteria or thick and tough called capsule in others.
Cell wall	▪ Determine the shape of the bacteria cell. ▪ Provide strong structural support to prevent bursting and collapsing of the bacterial cell. ▪ It is made up of peptidoglycan.
Plasma membrane	▪ Structurally similar to the eukaryotic cell. ▪ Semi-permeable and capable of interacting with the outside world.

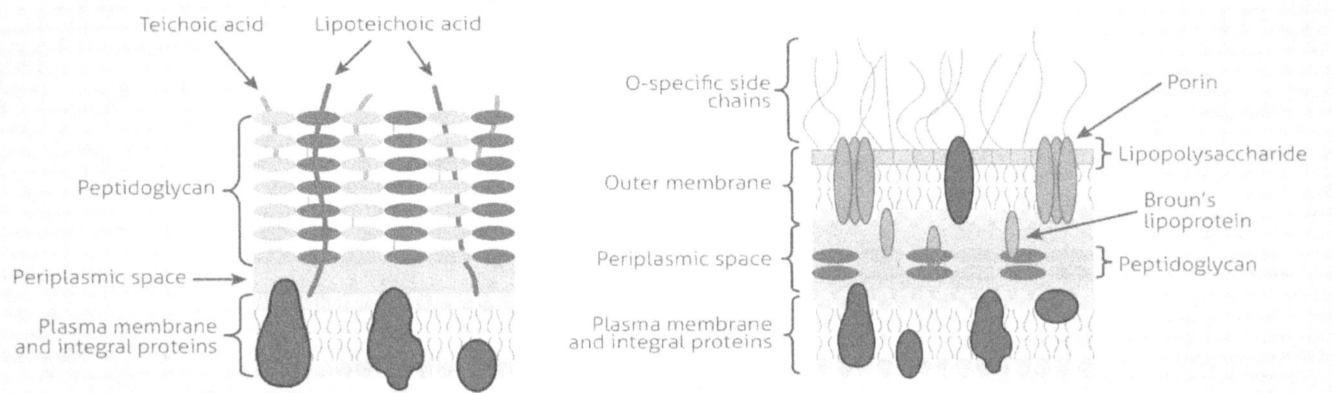

Figure 7: Cell Envelope Gram (+) and Gram (-) Bacteria

Do You Know 

Types of Bacterial Flagella

> ➤ The number and distribution of flagella varies in bacteria. Based on the number and position of flagella, bacteria, can be of the following types:
> 1. **Atrichous**: Flagella are absent. e.g., *Lactobacillus*.
> 2. **Monotrichous**: Single polar flagellum presents e.g., *Vibrio cholera*
> 3. **Amphitrichous**: Single flagellum present on both sides e.g., *Nitrosomonas*.
> 4. **Cephalotrichous**: A tuft of flagella present at one end. e.g., *Pseudomonas*.
> 5. **Lophotrichous**: Tuft of flagella present at both ends e.g., *Spirillum*
> 6. **Peritrichous**: Numerous flagella are present all over the bacterial body e.g., *Salmonella typhi*.

Cyclosis

> ➤ It is the process of protoplasmic streaming within a living cell without causing any deformation to the cell membrane. It is seen in fungal and plant cells e.g., Staminal hair of *Tradescantia*.

Modification	Description
Mesosome	<ul><li>Special membranous structure is formed by the extensions of the plasma membrane into the cell (infoldings).</li><li>The infoldings are in the form of vesicles, tubules, and lamellae.</li><li>Help in cell formation, DNA replication, and distribution to daughter cells, increasing the surface area of the plasma membrane and enzymatic content, respiration, and secretion.</li></ul>
Chromatophores	<ul><li>Membranous extensions into cytoplasm are found in some prokaryotes e.g., cyanobacteria.</li><li>Contain pigments such as chlorophyll.</li></ul>
Flagella	<ul><li>These are filamentous extensions of the cell wall.</li><li>Found in motile bacteria and help in locomotion.</li><li>Composed of three parts-filaments, hook, and the basal body.</li><li>The filament is the longest portion that extends to the exterior from the cell surface.</li><li>Number and arrangement of flagella in bacteria can vary.</li></ul>
Pili/sex pili	<ul><li>Elongated tubular structures on the surface of gram-negative bacteria.</li><li>Contains a special protein.</li><li>Shorter and thinner than flagella.</li><li>Pili develops in response to F^+ or fertility factor in gram-negative bacteria.</li></ul>
Fimbriae	<ul><li>Small bristle-like fibre, found in large numbers extending out of the cell.</li><li>In some bacteria they help in attaching the bacteria to rock streams and also to host tissues.</li></ul>

7.2 Ribosomes

- In prokaryotic cells, the ribosomes are associated with the plasma membrane.
- Each ribosome is about 15-20 nm in size.
- Ribosome is 70S.
- It is made up of two subunits-larger 50S and smaller 30S.
- Ribosomes are the site of protein synthesis.
- Many ribosomes can attach to a single mRNA to form a chain called polyribosomes or polysome.
- The ribosomes of a polysome translate mRNA into proteins.

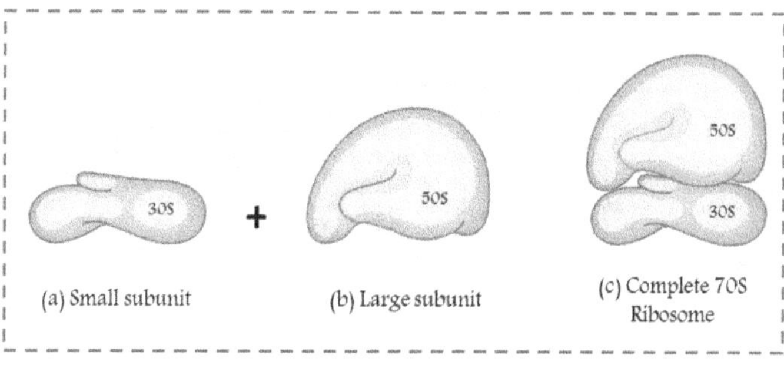

Figure 8: Prokaryotic Ribosome

7.3 Inclusion bodies

- These are the sites of storage of reserve materials in prokaryotic cells inside the cytoplasm.
- They are not membrane bound and lie freely in the cytoplasm.
- Example phosphate granules, cyanophycean granules, glycogen granules.
- Gas vacuoles are found in blue-green, purple and green photosynthetic bacteria.

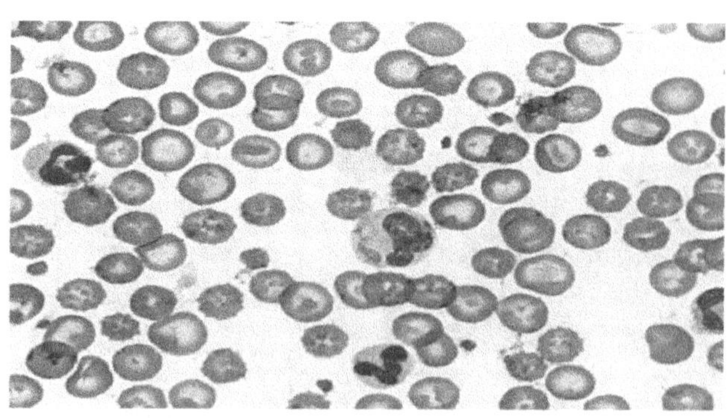

Figure 9: Inclusion body

- The eukaryotes include protists, fungi, plants and animals.
- Eukaryotic cells have an extensive compartmentalization of cytoplasm through the presence of several membrane bound organelles.
- All eukaryotic cells are not identical.
- On the other hand, animal cells have centrioles which are absent in plant cells.
- They have a membrane bound nucleus with a nuclear envelope and the genetic material is organized into chromosome.
- Eukaryotic cells also have a variety of complex locomotory and cytoskeletal structure.
- Plant and animal cells are different as the former possess cell walls, plastids and a large central vacuole which are absent in animal cells.

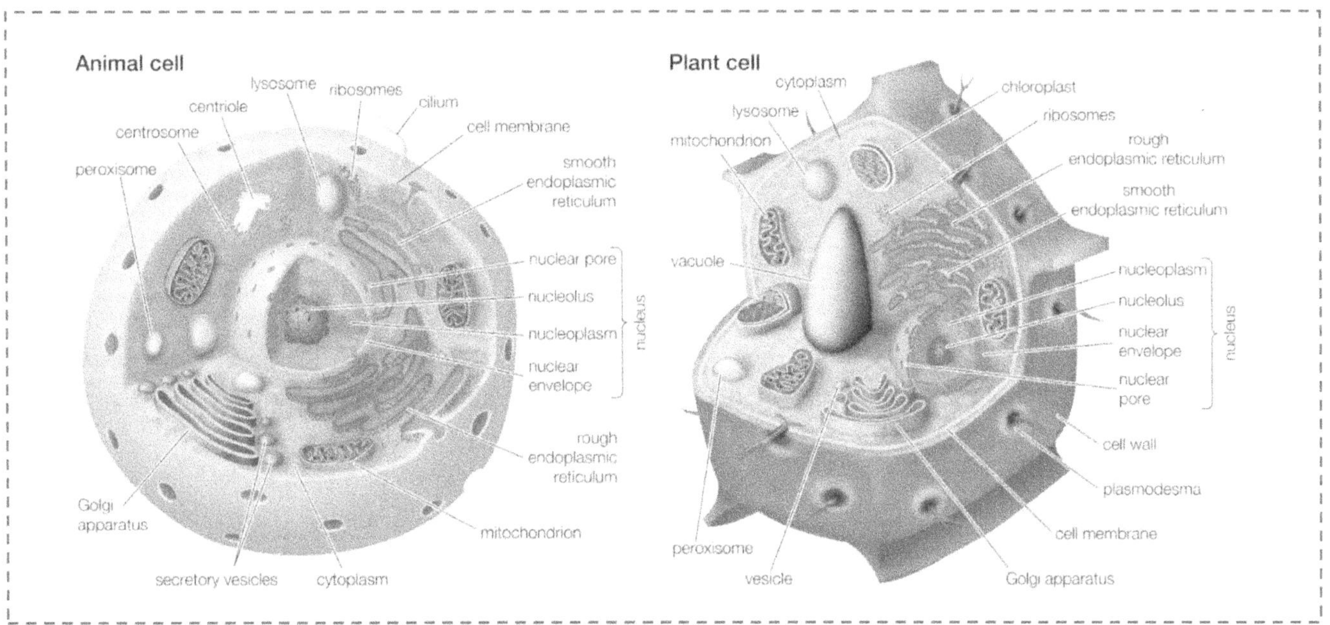

Figure 10: Diagram showing plant cell and animal cell

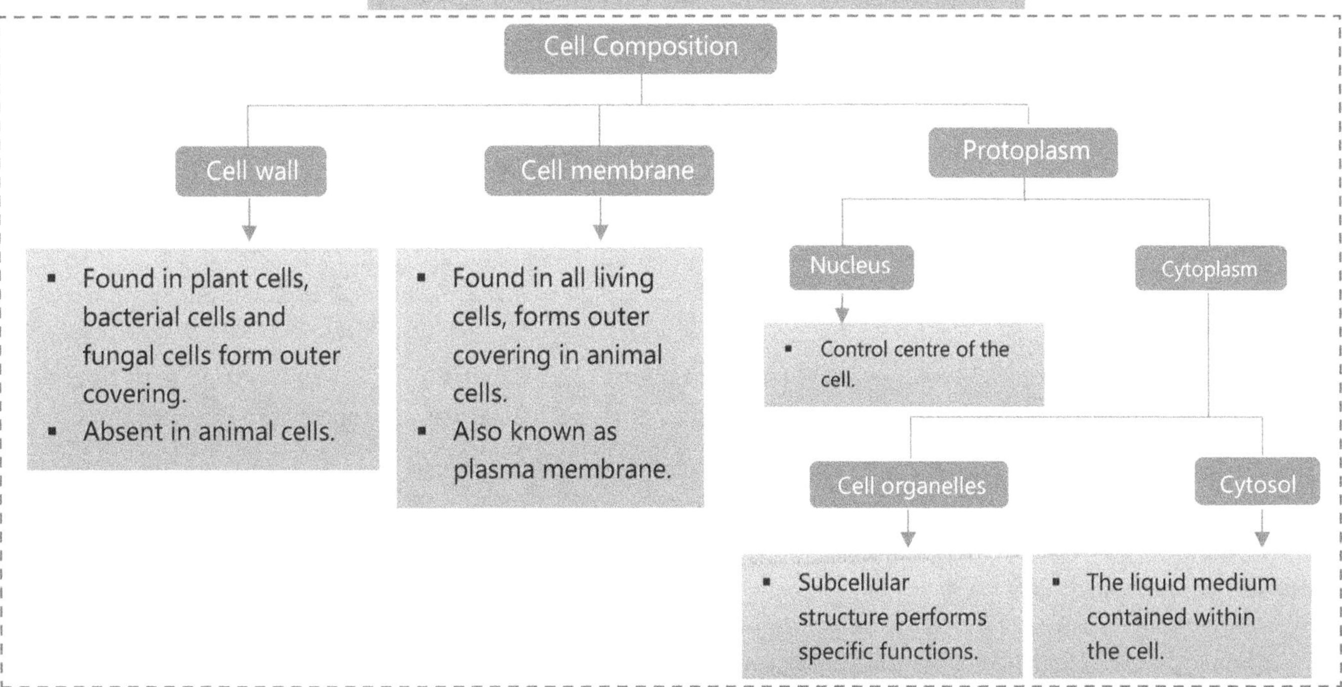

Figure 11: Composition of cells

- It is a non-living, rigid structure that forms the outer covering in fungi and plant cells.
- It is absent in animal cells.

8.1.1 Composition

- Cell wall of algae is made up of cellulose, galactans and mannans. It also consists of minerals like calcium carbonates.
- Cell wall of other higher plants consists of cellulose, hemicellulose, pectin and proteins.
- Cell wall in fungus is made up of chitin.

8.1.2 Structure

- A mature plant cell wall has the following three layers:

1) Middle lamella
    - It is outermost layer of the cell wall.
    - It mainly consists of calcium pectate and magnesium pectate.
    - It holds or glues neighbouring cells together.

2) Primary cell wall
    - It is present inner middle lamella.
    - It is a thin and elastic layer capable of growth.
    - It is composed of 2-5% cellulose, 50% hemicellulose, pectic polysaccharides and glycoprotein.
    - Meristematic and parenchymatous cells have only primary cell wall.
    - As the cell matures, it gradually diminishes and the secondary cell wall is formed towards the inner side.

3) Secondary cell wall
    - It is present inner to primary cell wall and outside the plasma membrane.
    - It consists of 50-90% cellulose, 5-25% hemicellulose, xylan and lignin.
    - The increased cellulose content makes thin layer non elastic and rigid.
    - Collenchyma, sclerenchyma and xylem vessels show presence of secondary cell wall.
    - Plasmodesmata are present in plant cell walls. They form channels for linking the cytoplasm of neighbouring cells.
    - Plasmodesmata consist of protoplasmic strands made up of fine tubules called **desmo tubes**.

8.1.3 Functions

- It gives shape of cell.
- Protect the cell from mechanical damage and infection.
- Helps in cell-to-cell interaction through plasmodesmata.
- Provides a barrier to undesirable macromolecule.

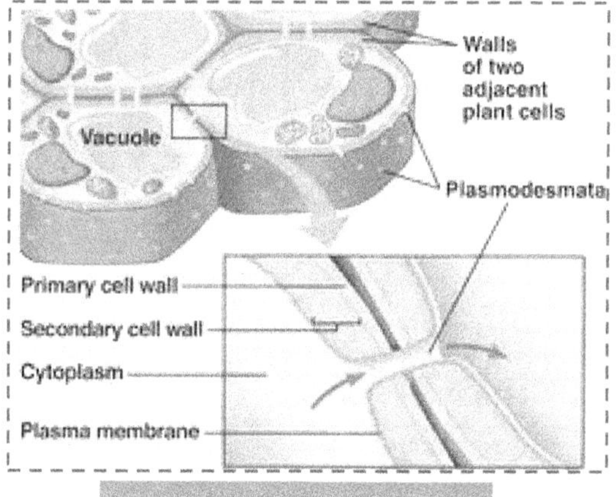

Figure 12: Plant cell wall

Supplementary Knowledge 

Discovery of cell wall

- When Robert Hooke observed the honeycomb structures of cork cells, he was actually looking at dead cells having non-living cell walls. A mature cork cells is non-living. The cell walls are composed of a waxy and impermeable substance called **suberin**.

Pits

- Certain areas of the cell wall lack secondary walls. Such unthicken regions are known as **pits**.

Smaller unit of plant cell wall

- Cellulose is the major constituent of plant cell wall. Each cellulose chain is composed of around 2000-2500 glucose units. About 100 such cellulose chains are arranged in parallel to form a micelle to form a miracle which is the smallest structural unit of cell wall.

8.2 Cell membrane

- It is also known as the plasma membrane or plasmalemma.
- The term cell membrane was given by **C. Nageli**, and **C. Kramer**.
- The term plasmalemma was given by **J. Q. Plower**.
- It is delicate, elastic, selectively permeable and living.
- Detailed study of the structure of the cell membrane became possible after the advent of the electron microscope in the 1950s.
- Chemical studies on cell membrane, especially in human red blood cells (RBCs) was done by scientists.

8.2.1 Composition

- The cell membrane is made up of three components- proteins, lipids, and carbohydrates.
- The lipids of the membrane mainly consist of phosphoglycerides i.e., phospholipids.
- The membrane proteins are classified into two types on the basis of ease of extraction- Peripheral proteins and integral proteins.

- The protein and lipid ratio varies considerably in different types of cells e.g., human RBCs have 52% protein and 40% lipids.

8.2.2 Structure

- The cell membrane is composed of a lipid bilayer revealed by the study of RBCs.
- Each lipid molecule consists of a polar head (hydrophilic) placed towards the outside and two non-polar (hydrophobic) tails towards the inner side of the membrane.
- In addition, phospholipid membrane also contains cholesterol.
- This orientation protects the non-polar tail of saturated hydrocarbons from the aqueous environment.
- Study of biochemicals later revealed the presence of proteins and carbohydrates in the membrane.
- Peripheral proteins lie on the membrane surface whereas integral proteins are partially or totally embedded in the membrane.
- **S. J. Singer** and **J. Nicholson** proposed a model (**Fluid mosaic model**) for plasma membrane structure.

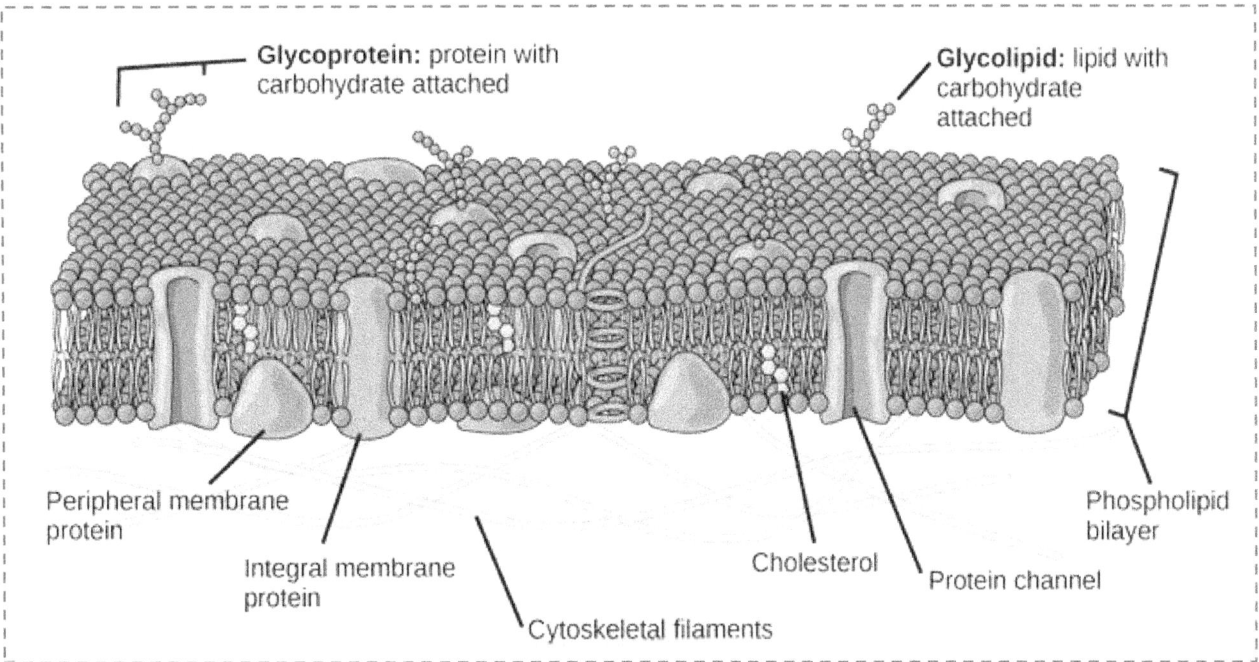

Figure 13: Fluid mosaic model of Plasma membrane

8.2.3 Fluid mosaic model or quasi-fluid model

- This model was proposed by **S. J. Singer** and **G. Nicholson** in 1972 to explain the arrangement of membrane constituents.
- The fluid mosaic model was an improved model and widely accepted.
- Before this model, Davson-Denielli proposed the **sandwich** or **lamellar model** or **Davson-Denielli model** of the plasma membrane in 1935 which proposed that a lipid layer is **sandwiched** between two protein layers in the membrane.
- According to the fluid mosaic model the membrane structure consists of a bilayer of lipids in which membrane proteins are embedded.
- Plasma membrane range from 5-10 nm in thickness.
- The main fabric of the membrane is composed of amphiphilic or dual-loving, phospholipid molecules.
- The hydrophilic or water-loving areas of these molecules are in contact with the aqueous fluid both inside and outside the cell. Hydrophobic, or water-hating molecules, tend to be non-polar.
- A phospholipid molecule consists of a three-carbon glycerol backbone with two fatty acid molecules attached to carbons 1 and 2 and a phosphate-containing group attached to the third carbon.
- This arrangement gives the overall molecule an area described as its **head** (the phosphate-containing group), which has a polar character or negative charge, and an area called **the tail** (the fatty acids), which has no charge.
- They interact with other non-polar molecules in chemical reactions, but generally do not interact with polar molecules. When placed in water, hydrophobic molecules tend to form a ball or cluster.
- The hydrophilic regions of the phospholipids tend to form hydrogen bonds with water and other polar molecules on both the exterior and interior of the cell.
- The phospholipid molecules move rapidly in their own layers thereby providing fluidity.
- Most of the protein molecules float in the phospholipid bilayer forming a fluid mosaic pattern.
- The movement of lipids from one lipid monolayer to another is known as **flip-flop movement**. This movement is rare in comparison to lateral movement i.e., within the same layer.
- Carbohydrates, the third major component of plasma membranes, are always found on the exterior surface of cells where they are bound either to proteins (forming glycoproteins) or to lipids (forming glycolipids).

8.2.4 Functions

- Transport process can be active or passive.
- In passive transport, molecules can move across the membrane without any requirement of energy e.g., neural solutes and water move through simple diffusion from a region of higher concentration to region of lower concentration i.e., along the concentration gradient.
- In active transport, certain ions and molecules are transported against concentration gradient i.e., form a region of lower concentration to higher concentration e.g., **Na⁺/K⁺ pump**.
- Active transport requires energy in the form of ATP.
- Movement of water by diffusion across the semi permeable membrane is called **osmosis.**

Supplementary Knowledge

Membrane protein

- In plasma membrane there are two type of protein, extrinsic protein (surface protein) and integral protein (channel protein).
- Integral membrane proteins are also known as **transmembrane** or **intrinsic protein** whereas peripheral membrane proteins are also known as **extrinsic proteins**.

➤ Integral proteins are difficult to extract whereas peripheral proteins are easy to extract.

➤ Integral proteins constitute 70% of total membrane proteins while peripheral proteins constitute the remaining 30%.

➤ Integral proteins help in transfer of molecules across the bilayer. Peripheral proteins help in cell recognition and interaction.

➤ Certain molecules require a carrier protein of the membrane to facilitate their transfer e.g., polar molecules that cannot pass the non-polar lipid bilayer.

Sodium potassium ion pump (Na⁺ - K⁺ pump)

➤ The sodium potassium pump is an example of active transport across the membrane. The sodium ions are pumped out and potassium ions are pumped inside the membrane. This builds up a chemical and electrical gradient across the membrane of neurons.

❖ Cell organelles are divides on the basis of membrane:

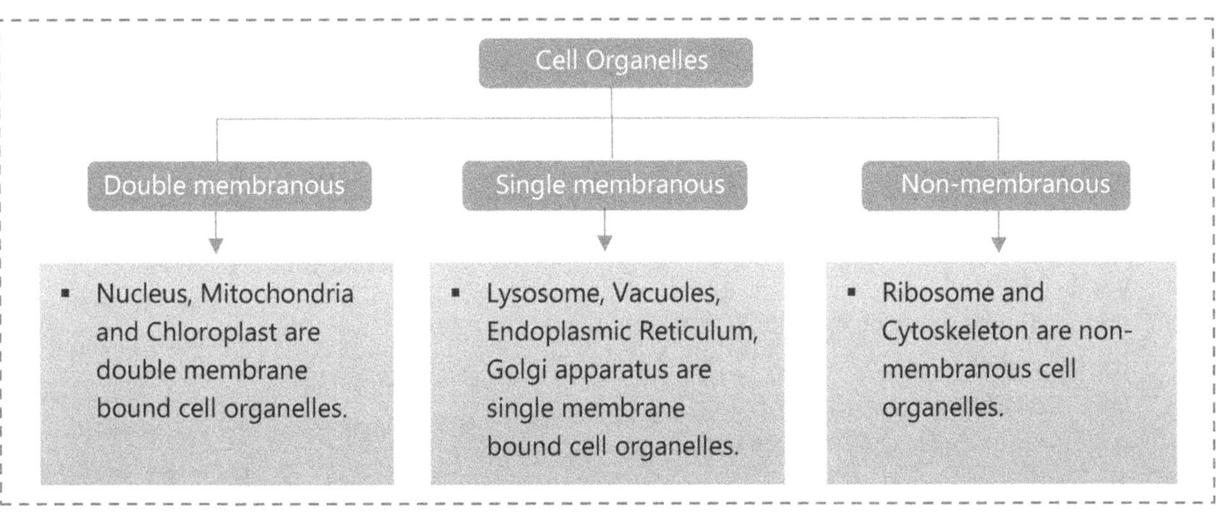

Figure 14: Types of organelles

8.3 Nucleus

- Nucleus was first described by **Robert Brown** in 1931 after observing orchid root cells.

- The genetic material inside the nucleus was later named chromatin by Flemming after staining them with basic dyes.

- The nucleus is a double membrane cell organelle that controls cellular metabolism & encloses the genetic information in the form of the chromosome.

- Generally, there is only one nucleus per cell but some organisms can have more than one nucleus also e.g., osteoclasts in bones.

- Some mature cells can be without a nucleus also e.g., RBCs of many mammals and sieve tube cells of many vascular plants.

8.3.1 Structure and functions

- The structure of the nucleus as observed under the electron microscope, reveals the following parts in a non-diving cell (during interphase):

1. **Nuclear membrane**

   ▪ It is also called the nuclear membrane.

   ▪ It consists of two parallel membranes i.e.; it is a double membrane structure.

   ▪ The space present between the two membranes is known as perinuclear space. It is 10-50 nm thick.

   ▪ The perinuclear space forms a barrier between the materials present inside the nucleus and that of the cytoplasm.

- The nuclear envelope has a number of pores that are formed by the fusion of two membranes.
- The outer nuclear membrane is continuous with the endoplasmic reticulum and contains ribosomes on its surface.
- The movement of RNA and protein molecules (in both directions) takes place between the nucleus and the cytoplasm through these nuclear pores.

2. Nucleoplasm

- The Nucleoplasm is also known as **Karyoplasm.**
- The Nucleoplasm is the nuclear matrix or the fluid part of the nucleus.
- It contains the nucleolus and chromatin fibers.

3. Nucleolus

- The nucleoli are spherical structures inside the nucleoplasm.
- Primary function is to produce and assemble the cell's ribosomes.
- It consists of RNA, DNA and proteins.
- It also transcribes Ribosomal RNA genes.
- The nucleolus is the site for active ribosomal RNA synthesis.
- Cells that are involved in active protein synthesis have larger and numerous nucleoli.

4. Chromatin

- Later the Material of the nucleus stained by basic dyes was given the name **Chromatin** by **Flemming** in 1880.
- An interphase nucleus shows a loose and indistinct network of nucleoprotein fibers called **Chromatin**.
- Chromatin consists of DNA along with basic proteins called **histone**, non-histone protein, and RNA.
- During cell division, the chromatin condenses and thickness to form specialized structures called **Chromosome.**

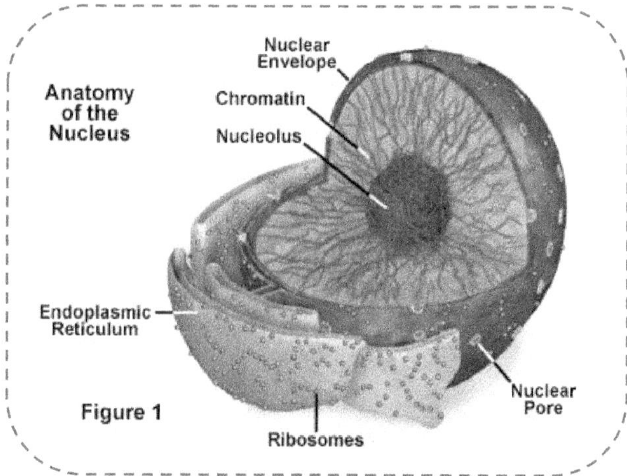

Figure 15: Structure of Nucleus

- Thus, during different stages of cell division, the chromosomes are visible instead of the nucleus.
- Every chromosome consists of a primary constriction or centromere on the sides of which disc-shaped structures called **kinetochores** are present.
- Chromosomes can be classified into four types based on the position of the centromere.
- Sometimes a few chromosomes have a non-staining secondary constriction at the constant location. This gives an appearance of a small fragment called that **satellite**.

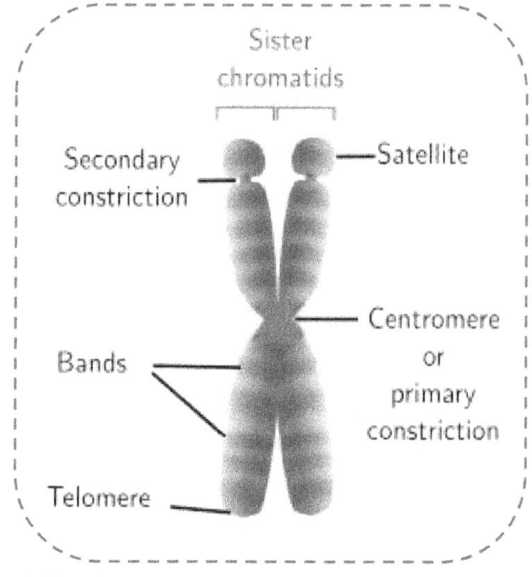

Figure 15: Structure of chromosomes

- In a cell of human, the number of chromosomes is forty-six, i.e., 23 pairs.
- If the DNA of all 46 chromosomes that are present in a single cell, will unwind and be attached to each other than the length of DNA become 2 meters.

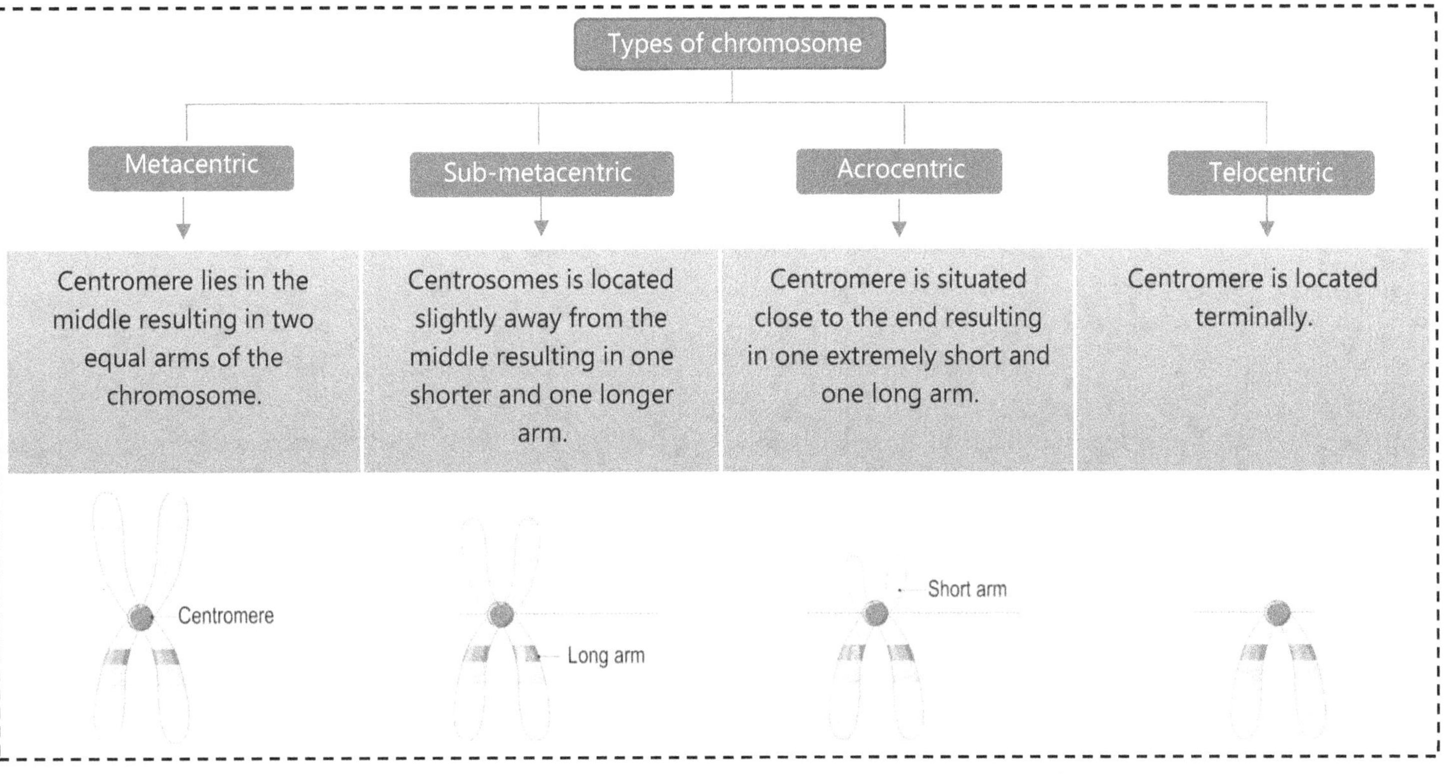

Figure 16: Types of chromosomes

Supplementary Knowledge 

Facts about nucleus

- The term chromosome was first used by German anatomist W. Waldeyer Hartz in 1988.
- The nuclear membrane is a derivative of the rough endoplasmic reticulum.
- Acentric chromosome-A chromosome without a centromere is known as acentric.

Giant Chromosome

1. Polytene/Salivary gland chromosome

- First time reported in 1881 by E. G. Balbiani in the salivary glands of *Chironomus* larva.
- These are giant chromosomes.
- These are found in the salivary glands, midgut epithelium, rectum and Malpighian tubules of larvae of certain insects e.g., *Drosophila, Sciaria* etc.
- These cells have large nucleus about 25μ in diameter. The chromosome is 50 – 200 times larger than the chromosomes in normal cells.
- Polytene chromosomes consists of numerous parallel chromatids appearing as strands which do not separate from one to another following duplication.
- The thread appears to radiate from a deeply stained structure called **chromosome**.
- Some specific regions on polytene chromosomes become uncoiled during larval development, forming localized regions called **puffs** or **Balbiani rings**. These regions are active regions where protein and RNA synthesized.

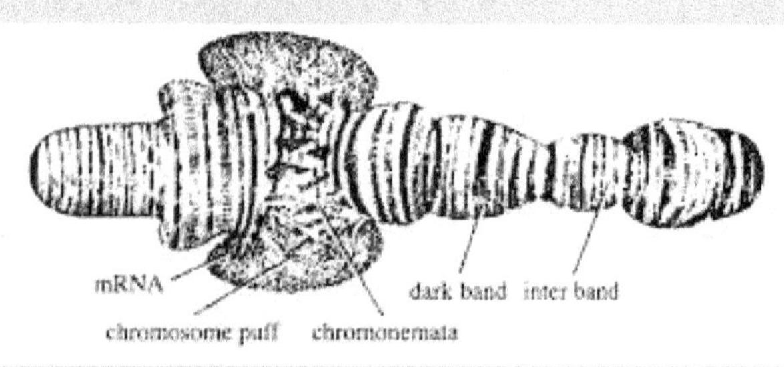

Figure 17: Structure of polytene chromosomes

2. Lampbrush Chromosome

> First time reported in 1982 by Flemming in oocytes of many invertebrates and all vertebrates except mammals.

> As they are so appearing like the brush used for cleaning chimneys when viewed under a light microscope.

> These are almost 3 times larger than polytene chromosomes.

> They are found in the diplotene phase of meiosis.

> They are extremely elastic and can be stretched two times their length.

> Each lampbrush chromosome has two parts-a main axis loops. Two chromatids are found at the main axis which extend in the form of loops. Synthesis of RNA and proteins take place in the loops.

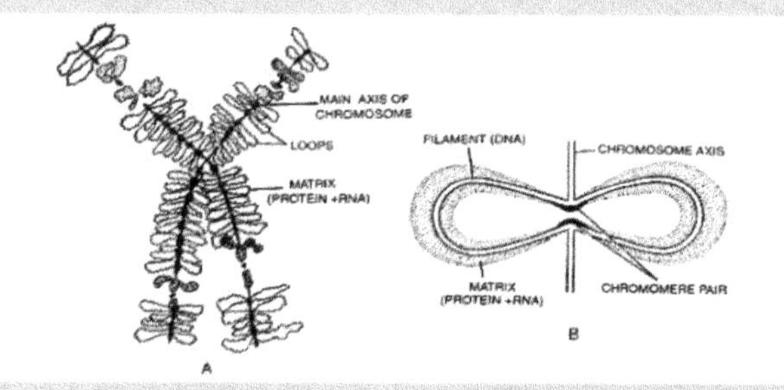

Figure 18: Structure of lampbrush chromosomes

8.4 Endomembrane system

- Each of the membranous organelles is distinct in the terms of its structure and function, many of these are considered together as an endomembrane system because their functions are coordinated.

- The endomembrane system includes endoplasmic reticulum (ER), Golgi complex, lysosomes and vacuoles.

- Since the functions of mitochondria, chloroplast, and peroxisomes are not coordinated with the above components, these are not considered as a part of endomembrane system.

8.4.1 Endoplasmic reticulum

- Endoplasmic reticulum was first reported by Porter, Claude, and Fullam in 1945.

- Electron microscopic studies of eukaryotic cells reveal the presence of a network or reticulum of tiny tubular structures scattered in the cytoplasm which is the Endoplasmic reticulum.

- It is a network of double membrane-bound tubular structures scattered around in the cytoplasm.

- It extends from the nucleus to the plasma membrane, crossing the cytoplasm.

- It is poorly developed in rapidly dividing cells.

- Therefore, the endoplasmic reticulum (ER) divides the intracellular space into two distinct compartments:

  > Luminal (inside ER) compartment.

  > Extra luminal (cytoplasm) compartment.

8.4.1 Composition and Structure

- The ER membrane is thinner than the plasma membrane and consists of lipids.

- They may or may not have ribosomes attached to their outer surface.

- The ER can have the following shapes:

  - Cisternae: Broad, flat membrane-bound space arranged in parallel and associated with ribosomes.

  - Tubules: tubes like structures without ribosomes.

  - Vesicles: Round or oval isolated sacs also without ribosomes.

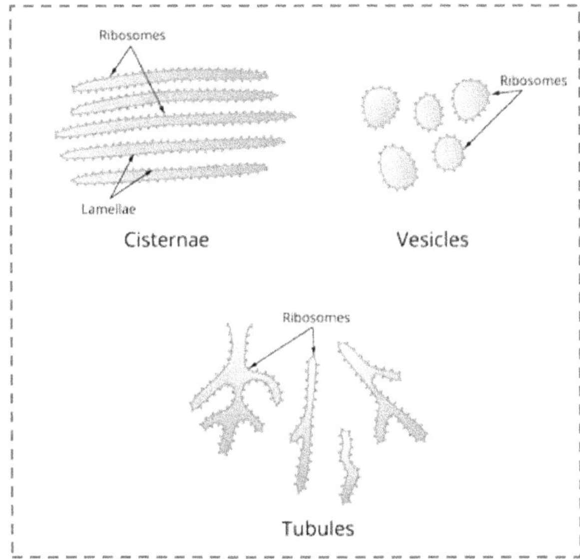

8.4.2 Types

- Based on whether ribosomes are attached or not to their surface, ER can be two types:
- Rough Endoplasmic Reticulum (RER)
    - It bears ribosomes on the surface of which makes the surface look rough.
    - They are extensive and continuous with the outer nuclear membrane.
    - Consist of cisternae.
- Smooth Endoplasmic Reticulum (SER)
    - Does not bear ribosomes on the surface

Supplementary Knowledge 

- ➢ Rough ER is the major site of protein synthesis. Modification of proteins such as glycosylation takes place in the endoplasmic reticulum. It is responsible for routing the newly synthesized proteins to their destination.
- ➢ The membrane of smooth ER contains enzymes for catalysing reactions for detoxification; of lipids drugs and other harmful compounds e.g., enzymes of the cytochrome P450 family.
- ➢ Liver cells or hepatocytes have a large amount of smooth ER for detoxification.
- ➢ Nissl's granules are found in neurons. These granules are formed from RER and more the sites of protein synthesis.

therefore, give a smooth look to the surface.
- Mainly consist of tubules and vesicles.

8.4.3 Functions

- RER is found in cells actively involved in protein synthesis and secretion.
- SER is the major site for lipid synthesis.
- Steroidal hormones having lipid like structures are synthesized by SER in animals.
- ER provides mechanical support to the cells by dividing the intracellular space into compartments.
- SER helps in detoxification.

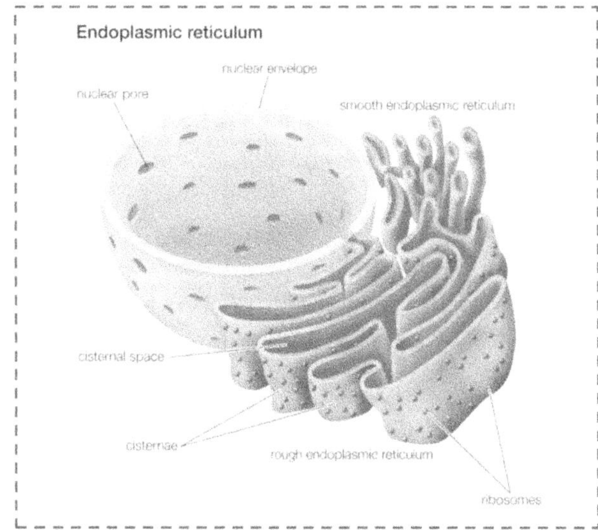

8.4.2 Golgi Apparatus

- **Camillo Golgi** first observed them in 1898 as densely stained reticular structures near the nucleus.
- The Golgi apparatus consists of many flat, disc-shaped, membrane-bound sacs called **cisternae**.
- Golgi apparatus is present near the rough endoplasmic reticulum and near the nucleus at the perinuclear area.

8.4.2.1 Structure

- The diameter of cisternae lies between 0.5 μm to 1μm.
- The cisternae are stacked parallel to each other.

- They are formed continuously at one end and bud off as vesicles at the other end.
- The number of cisternae present in a Golgi apparatus varies.
- The Golgi cisternae are arranged concentrically near the nucleus.
- They have a distinct convex *cis* or forming face and a concave *trans* or maturing face.
- These two faces are different but interconnected to each other.
- Apart from cisternae, the Golgi apparatus also consists of tubules and vesicles.
- Tubules are small, flat structures arising from the periphery of the cisternae.
- Vesicles are large round structures found on the edge of the *cis* and *trans* face.
- Plant and fungal cells have a single stack of Golgi apparatus called dictyosome.

8.4.2.2 Functions

- The main function of the Golgi apparatus is secretion, and packing transportation, i.e., materials are packed to be delivered to either intracellular targets or secreted outside the cell.
- Materials to be packaged in the form of vesicles from the ER fuse with the *cis* face and move towards the *trans* face.
- Also, many proteins synthesized by the ribosomes attached to RER are modified in Golgi cisternae before releasing from *trans* face.
- Therefore, ER and Golgi apparatus remain in close association.

8.4.3 Lysosome

- It was first reported by **Christian de Duve** in 1955.
- They were formed through the process of packaging inside the Golgi apparatus.

8.4.3.1 Structure

- These are single membrane-bound structures.
- The isolated lysosomal vesicles are rich in all types of hydrolytic enzymes (hydrolases) i.e., carbohydrase, proteases, and lipases.

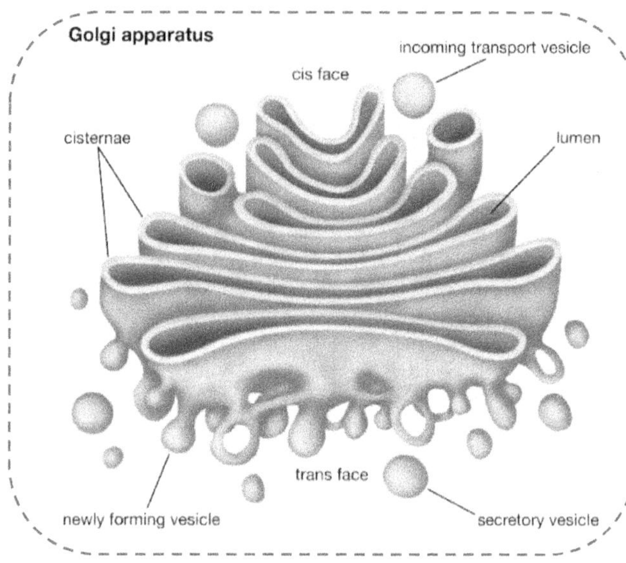

Figure 21: Golgi Apparatus

- Golgi apparatus is also the site of synthesis of glycoproteins and glycolysis.
- Golgi apparatus also helps in the synthesis of carbohydrates, hormones, cell walls, lysosomes, pigments, and acrosomes.

Supplementary Knowledge 

- ➤ Golgi apparatus was discovered by Camilo Golgi. He wanted to study the central nervous system by staining the nerve cells (Purkinje cells) of the cerebellum of an owl.
- ➤ He noticed thread-like networks inside the cells which he named *apparato reticolare interno (internal reticular apparatus)*.
- ➤ It is a term used to refer to the Golgi apparatus.

- Lysosomes contain the enzyme acid phosphatase.
- These enzymes are optimally active at acidic pH.
- The hydrolases enable the lysosomes to digest the cell itself due to which they have been named as suicidal bags on the garbage system of a cell.

8.4.3.2 Functions

- The lysosomal enzymes can digest carbohydrates, lipids, proteins, and nucleic acids.

- Lysosomes digest incoming food materials and remove foreign particles, toxins and debris.
- Intracellular digestion occurs through autophagy (self-eating) and heterophagy (eating other substances).
- Heterophagosome is formed by fusion of primary lysosome with food containing phagosome.
- Lysosomes help in the renewal of worn-out cells and organelles.

Supplementary Knowledge 

Polymorphism in lysosomes

- Lysosomes exhibit polymorphism. i.e., they exist in multiple forms which include:
  - **(a) Primary lysosomes:** They are formed from ER and Golgi apparatus.
  - **(b) Secondary lysosomes:** They are formed from the fusion of food-containing vesicles called **phagosomes** and enzymes containing lysosomes.
  - **(c) Residual bodies:** They are lysosomes containing indigestible materials.
  - **(d) Autophagic vacuoles:** They are formed around degenerated cells or organelle.

GERL system

- The GERL system is a complex comprised of Golgi apparatus, endoplasmic reticulum, and lysosome.
- These organelles form a system to carry out the processes of endocytosis, exocytosis, synthesis or recycling of materials, and removal of wastes.

Endocytosis

- Endocytosis is the process of capturing a particle or substance by engulfing it with the cell membrane to bring it inside the cell from outside.

Exocytosis

- Exocytosis is the process of fusion of vesicles with the plasma membrane to release their contents outside the cell.

Few useful facts

- Phagocytosis was first seen by Metchnikoff.
- Disappearance of tadpole tail during metamorphosis is brought about by lysosomes.

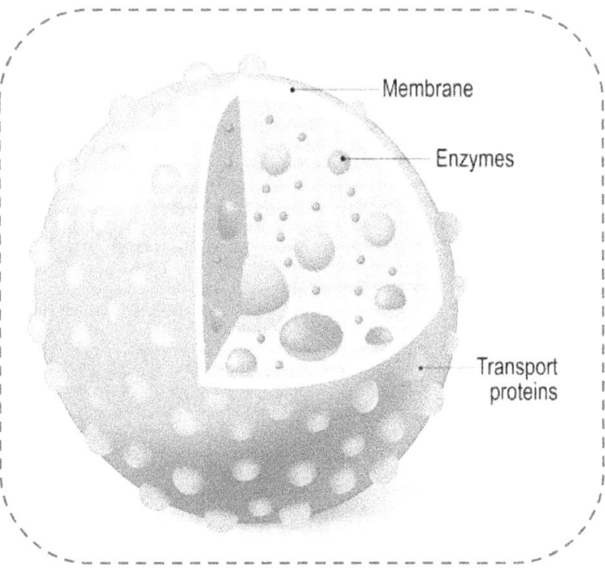

Figure 22: Lysosome

8.4.4 Vacuoles

- Vacuoles were first time reported by **Felix Dujardin** in 1835.
- Vacuoles are single membrane-bound spaces found in the cytoplasm.
- In plant cells vacuoles can occupy 90% of the cell volume.
- Large in plant and fungal cells but small in animal cells.

8.4.4.1 Structure

- Vacuoles are bound by a single membrane called **tonoplast**.
- Vacuoles contain water, the cell sap, excretory products, and other materials that are not useful for the cells.
- The cell sap has high osmotic pressure which helps in creating turgor pressure in plant cells.

8.4.4.2 Types

- The various types of vacuoles are:
  - **Sap vacuoles** contain dissolved salts and maintain turgor pressure in plant cells.
  - **Contractile vacuoles**-Helps in osmoregulation and excretion, e.g., *Amoeba*.

- **Food vacuoles**-formed by engulfing food particles, e.g., in protists. They contain hydrolases for the digestion of food.
- **Gas vacuoles**-Contains air and provides buoyancy to bacteria. They are found in green bacterial cells.

8.4.4.3 Functions

- Storage of substances including waste products of cells.
- In plant cells the tonoplast helps in the transfer of ions and other materials against the concentration gradient into the vacuole.
- Concentration inside the vacuoles is higher than cytoplasm.

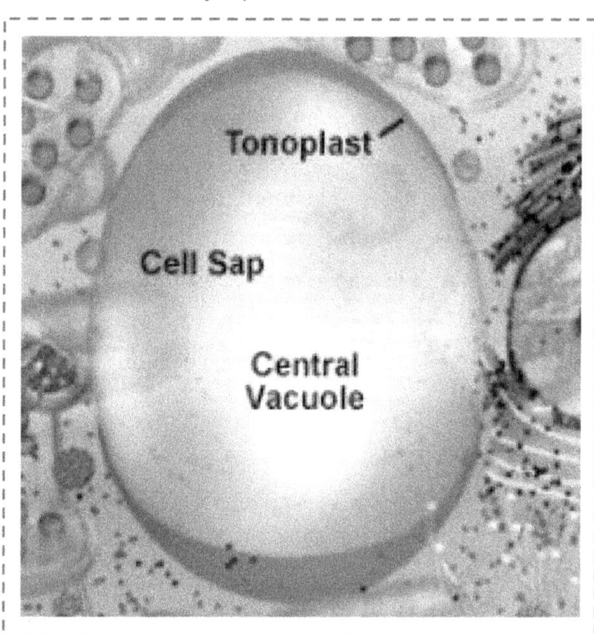

Figure 23: Vacuoles

Supplementary Knowledge 

Pigments in Vacuoles

- Many plant vacuoles contain water-soluble pigments called **anthocyanins**.
- These pigments give the red and blue colours to vegetables e.g., turnips, beetroot, radish, and cabbages; fruits e.g., cherries, plums, and grapes; and flowers e.g., geraniums, roses, etc. The cell membrane is impermeable to anthocyanin.

Sphaerosomes

- These are single membrane-bound organelles called **microbodies.**
- They are found in plant cells. They are spherical vesicles formed from smooth endoplasmic reticulum.
- Their main function is synthesis and storage of lipids. They contain enzymes such as nucleases,

Peroxisomes

- These are also microbodies. They occur mainly in the leaves of C_3 plants. Hydrolysis of H_2O_2 into H_2O and O_2 takes place inside peroxisomes. This process is called **peroxidation**. It is a method of detoxification of cells. They also play a role in photorespiration.
- They are also involved in the oxidation of amino acids and uric acid. They contain enzymes such as catalase, urease, oxidase, etc.
- Recent research suggests that peroxisomes have an actinobacterial origin. Peroxisomes also help in glycolate metabolism.

Glyoxysomes

- These are also microbodies that help in converting fats into carbohydrates. They contain enzymes necessary for the production of intermediate products for the synthesis of sugars by the process of gluconeogenesis. They are found in the endosperm of germinating seeds.

8.5 Mitochondria

- Mitochondria was first reported by physiologist Albert von Kolliker in 1857 and were named by Carl Benda in 1897.
- Mitochondria (single mitochondrion) are the sites of aerobic respiration, a process involving the oxidation of nutrients to generate energy.
- They are known as the powerhouse of the cell as they produce energy in the form of ATP.
- Mitochondria divide by binary fission and they contain their own single-stranded, circular DNA.

- Their number inside the cell depends on the physiological activity of the cells.
- They are most abundant in actively metabolizing cells and tissues.
- They need to be specifically stained for viewing under the microscope.
- They are absent in mature RBCs.

8.5.1 Composition and structure

- It consists of 70% protein and 30% lipids.
- These are typically sausage-shaped or cylindrical.
- The diameter ranges from 0.2 μm to 1 μm with an average of 0.5 μm.
- The length of mitochondria can be between 1 μm to 4.1 μm.
- It is a double membranous structure.
- The outer membrane forms a continuous limiting boundary whereas the inner membrane forms infoldings called **cristae** (sing. Crista) that increase the surface area.
- The two surfaces have specific enzymes for particular functions.
- The membranes divide the lumen distinctly into two aqueous compartments-the outer and inner compartments.
- The inner compartment is called a **matrix**.
- The matrix contains the DNA molecule, a few RNA molecules, 70S ribosomes, and components necessary for the synthesis of protein.
- Due to the presence of the above, mitochondria are called **semi-autonomous** organelles.

8.5.2 Functions

- Cellular respiration through oxidative phosphorylation i.e., ATP formation through Krebs' cycle and electron transport chain (ETC).
- Cristae are the sites of under electron transport chain whereas matrix is the site of Krebs' cycle (also called **TCA cycle**)
- The intermediate products of cellular respiration are used in the formation of steroids, cytochromes, chlorophyll, nucleic acids, amino acids, etc.

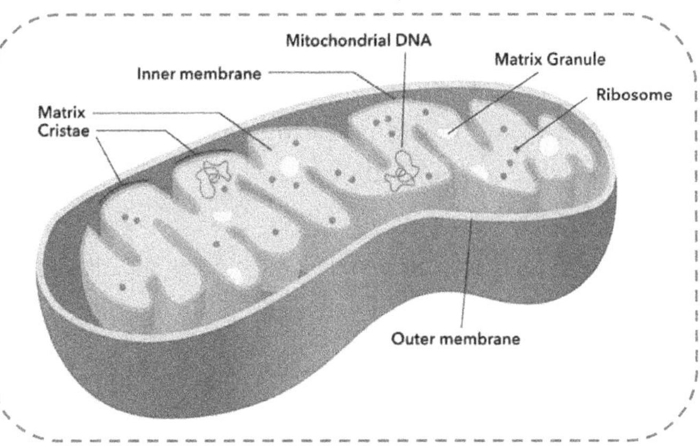

Figure 24: L.S of Mitochondria

Supplementary Knowledge 

Mitochondria cristae and respiration

- ➤ The inner mitochondrial membrane (cristae) is the site of the electron transport chain.
- ➤ They have the presence of F0 and F1 particles (also called **oxysomes, Parson's particles, Fernandez-Moran** particles, **ATP** synthetase or ATP synthase), ATPase, and TCA enzymes.

Mitoplast

- ➤ A mitochondrion without the outer membrane is called a **mitoplast**.
- ➤ It contains only the inner membrane and the matrix.

8.6 Plastids

- The term plastid was introduced by Ernst Haeckel in 1866.
- Plastids are organelles found in plant cells and euglenoids.
- They are absent in animal cells.
- Their large size enables them to be observed easily under the microscope.
- Plastids contain specific pigments that impart specific colors to plants.
- Their large size enables them to be observed easily under the microscope.
- Plastids contain specific pigments that impart specific colors to plants.

- Their large size enables them to be observed easily under the microscope.
- Plastids contain specific pigments that impart specific colors to plants.

8.6.1 Types

- Based on the type of pigments, plastids can be classified into three types:
    - Chloroplast
    - Chromoplast
    - Leucoplast

8.6.2 Chloroplast

- The term chloroplast was coined by **Sachimpor** in 1833.
- Most of the chloroplasts in green plants are located in the mesophyll cells of the leaves.
- Shape of the chloroplasts can be oval, spherical, discoid, ribbon-like, or lens-shaped.
- Their length varies between 5 μm to 10 μm and width varies between 2 μm to 4 μm.
- The number of chloroplasts is variable in different cells, e.g., green alga *Chlamydomonas* has only one whereas the mesophyll of the green plant can have 20-40 chloroplasts.

8.6.3 Structure

- Chloroplasts are double-membrane structures containing an outer and an inner membrane.
- The inner chloroplast membrane is less permeable than the outer membrane.
- The space limited by the inner membrane is called **stroma** or **stromal space**.
- The stroma contains a number of organized flattened membranous sacs called **thylakoids**.
- Chlorophyll pigment is present in the thylakoid membrane.
- The thylakoids are arranged in stacks like piles of coins called **grana** (Sing. Granum) or **integral thylakoids**.
- The thylakoids of different grana are connected by flat membranous tubules called **stromal lamella or inter grana.**
- The thylakoid membrane encloses a space called the **lumen**.
- The stroma contains enzymes necessary for the synthesis of carbohydrates and protein.
- Chloroplast also contains its own circular DNA in the stroma.
- Ribosomes are also found in the stroma. These ribosomes are smaller (70S) than the ribosomes in the cytoplasm (80S).
- Due to the presence of DNA and protein synthesis machinery, chloroplasts are also semi-autonomous like mitochondria.

Types of plastids	Pigment present	Colour imparted	Functions
1. **Chloroplast**	Chlorophyll, carotenoid	Green	Traps light energy thereby helping in process of photosynthesis.
2. **Chromoplast**	Fat-soluble catenoid pigments e.g., carotene, xanthophyll, etc.	Yellow, orange, or red	Imparts color flowers and fruits.
3. **Leucoplast**	Colorless plastids of various shapes and sizes.		Storage of nutrients. Can be further categorized into: a. Amyloplast-Store carbohydrates (starch) e.g., potato b. Elaioplats-Store fats and oils, e.g., tube rose c. Aleurone-Store proteins, e.g., aleurone layer of maize grain

Table 4: Types of plastids

8.6.4 Functions

- Major site of photosynthesis in green plants.
- Converts light energy into chemical energy.
- Maintain gaseous balance for photosynthesis i.e., intake of carbon dioxide and release of oxygen.

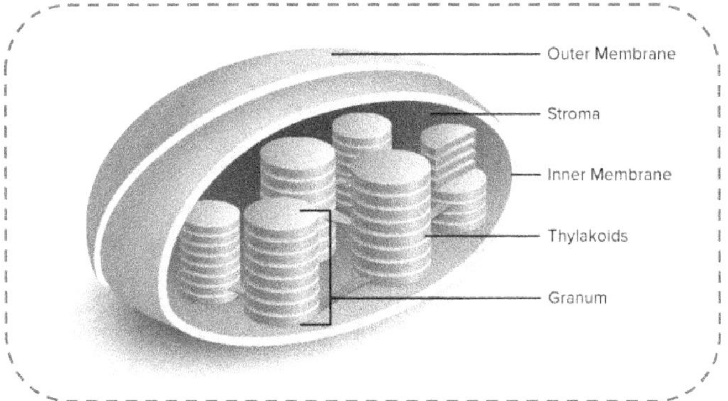

Figure 25: Structure of Chloroplast

Supplementary Knowledge 

Thylakoid

- The term thylakoid was coined by **Menke** in 1962 to describe the internal photosynthetic membranes of chloroplasts.
- Quantasomes are particles in the thylakoid membrane in which photosynthesis takes place.

The Endosymbiotic Theory

- The endosymbiotic theory is related to the origin of mitochondria and chloroplast. These two eukaryotic organelles are believed to have originated from symbiotic bacteria that were engulfed by a larger cell and subsequently become endosymbionts inside the larger cell. The two cells started living mutually. Over millions of years of evolution, mitochondria and chloroplasts have become more specialized and today they cannot live outside the cell.
- This theory is supported by the following evidence.
    - Both mitochondria and chloroplast have their own DNA.
    - Both mitochondria and chloroplast do not have to arise afresh (de novo).
    - Both mitochondria and chloroplast are double membranous structures. The inner membrane

of mitochondria is thrown into folds like the mesosome (prokaryotic cell infolding).
- Both mitochondria and chloroplast have 70S ribosomes like prokaryotes.
- Both mitochondria and chloroplast divide by binary fission like prokaryotes.

Agranal chloroplast

- Agranal chloroplast are found in some C_4 plants,

Chemical composition of chloroplast

- Chloroplasts contain 30-55% proteins, 20-30% lipids, 9% chlorophyll, 4-5% carotenoids, 3-7% RNA, and 0.5% DNA. They also have trace amounts of certain minerals.

8.7 Ribosomes

- Ribosomes were discovered by b in animal cells after he observed them as dense particles under an electron microscope in 1953.
- They are found in all cells that synthesize proteins.
- They either lie freely in the cytoplasm or are attached to a membrane e.g., in RER.
- The number of ribosomes in bacteria is around 1000 while in eukaryotes. It can range from one million to ten million.
- They are often called **RNA particles**.

8.7.1 Structure

- Ribosomes are made up of Ribonucleic Acid (RNA) and proteins.
- They are positively charged.
- These organelles are not bound by any membrane.
- The structure of ribosomes shows a large and a small subunit.
- Magnesium ions (Mg^{2+}) are necessary for the binding of the two subunits.
- Eukaryotic ribosomes are the 80S (combination of smaller subunit 40S and larger subunit 60S).
- Prokaryotic ribosomes are the 70S (combination of the smaller subunit 30S and larger subunit 50S).
- Svedberg's unit 'S' stands for sedimentation

coefficient. It is an indirect measure of density and size.

- Ribosomes may occur singly as monosomes or in groups with mRNA called **polysomes** in eukaryotes.

8.7.2 Functions

- Ribosomes are sites for protein synthesis.
- Ribosomes are attached to the membranes and are involved in the synthesis of secretory proteins, integral membrane proteins, peripheral proteins and lysosomal proteins.
- The free ribosomes are involved in the synthesis of soluble cytoplasmic proteins, peripheral mitochondrial proteins, chloroplast proteins, nuclear proteins, etc.
- The larger subunit contains the enzyme peptidyl transferase which is required for the formation of polypeptides.

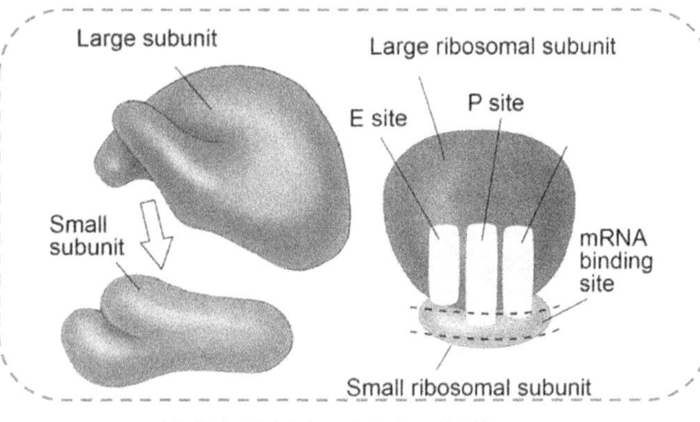

Figure 26: Ribosomes

Subdivision of Prokaryotic Ribosome

- ➢ 70S ribosome can be subdivided into 50S and 30S.
- ➢ 50S ribosomes consist of 5rRNA and 23S rRNA plus around 34 proteins.
- ➢ The 30S consists of 16S rRNA and 21 proteins.

8.8 Cytoskeleton

- Cytoskeleton is an elaborate network of filamentous structures found in the cytoplasm.
- All eukaryotic cells possess this crisscross network extending from the nucleus to the plasma membrane.

8.8.1 Structure

- The cytoskeleton is a dynamic system i.e., it keeps changing.
- There are three types of elements that make up the cytoskeleton-microtubules, microfilaments, and intermediate filaments.
- Microtubules were first discovered with the help of electron microscopy.

8.8.2 Functions

- Provide mechanical support to the cell.
- Maintains the shape of a cell.
- Helps in motility.
- Microtubules help in spindle formation during cell division.

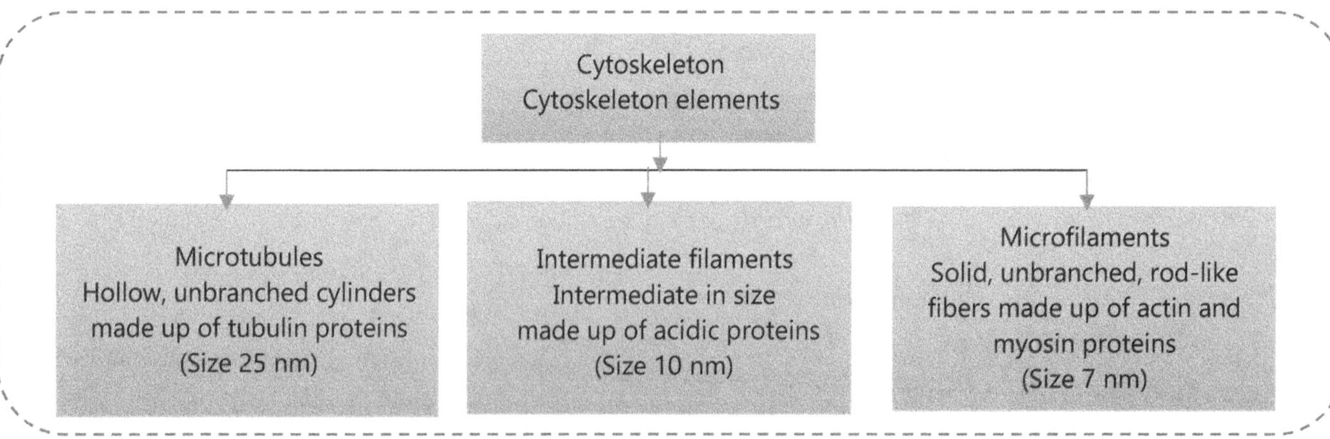

Figure 27: Types of elements in cytoskeleton

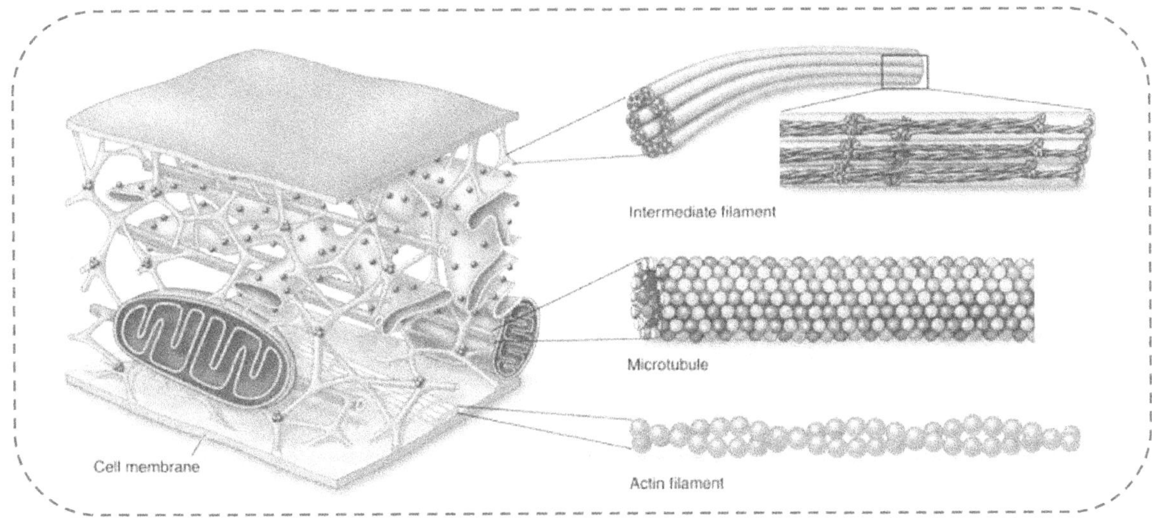

8.9 Cilia and flagella

- The cilia (sing. Cilium) and flagella (sing. Flagellum) are thin hair-like outgrowths extending from the cell membrane.
- The structure and functions of both cilia and flagella are similar.
- They can distinguish on the basis of their size and number. Flagella are longer and lesser in number whereas cilia are shorter and more in number.
- Flagella are found both in eukaryotic (bacterial) and eukaryotic cells, but they are structurally different from each other.

8.9.1 Structure

- The cilia and flagella consist of three parts:
    - Basal body,
    - Hook,
    - Filament.
- Electron microscope reveals that cilia and flagella are covered by the plasma membrane.
- The filament is a cylindrical structure. The core of cilia and flagella is known as the **axoneme**.
- Axoneme is made up of a number of microtubules running parallel to the long axis.
- The axoneme consists of nine pairs of duplets of radially arranged peripheral microtubules.
- It also has a pair of centrally located microtubules.
- On account of the arrangement of microtubules, it is referred to as the 9+2 array.

- The central microtubules are connected to each other by bridges.
- It is also enclosed by a central sheath which is connected to one of the tubules of each peripheral doublets by a radial spoke. Therefore, there are nine radial spokes in total.

8.9.2 Functions

- Both cilia and flagella help in locomotion.
- Cilia work like oars thereby helping in the movement of the cell or the surrounding fluid.
- Flagella help in the movement of the cell.

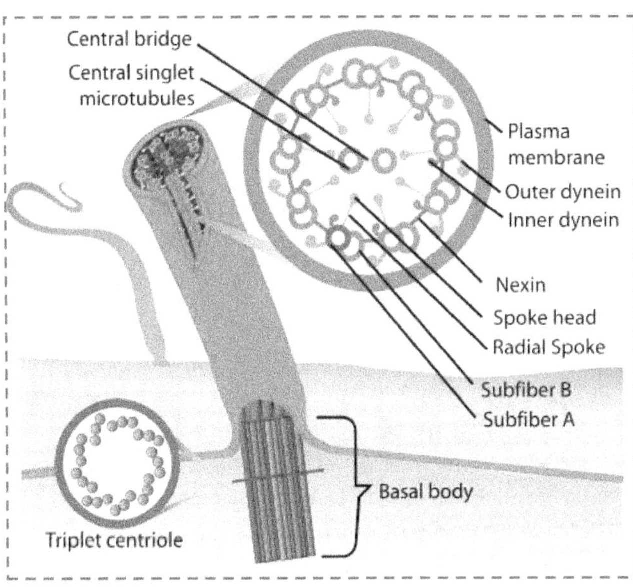

Figure 29: Section of cilia showing its parts: Diagrammatic representation of internal structure

- The term centrosome was introduced by **Boveri** in 1888.
- Centrosome is a cell organelle found in all animal cells, lower plants, and primitive flagellates.

8.9.1 Structure

- Centrosome contains two cylindrical, rod-shaped structures called **centrioles**.
- The two centrioles are together known as **diplosomes** and lie perpendicular to each other.
- Other centrioles are divided by amorphous pericentriolar materials.
- Each centriole has a cartwheel-like organization.
- Each centriole has two regions: Central and peripheral.
  - ❖ **Peripheral**
- The peripheral region contains nine evenly spaced peripheral fibrils of tubulin protein.
- Each peripheral fibril is a triplet having three sub-fibrils.

- The adjacent triplets are linked to each other forming a complete cylinder.
  - ❖ **Central**
- The central part of the proximal region is known as the **hub**.
- It is also proteinaceous in nature and consists of one or two longitudinally arranged strands.
- The hub is connected to the tubules of the peripheral triplet by radially spokes made up of protein.
- During cell division, the centrioles develop many radiating threads or rays and the complete structure is called **aster**.

8.9.2 Functions

- The centrioles form the basal body of cilia and flagella.
- Centrosome helps in the formation of spindle fibers that gives rise to spindle apparatus during cell division in animal cells.

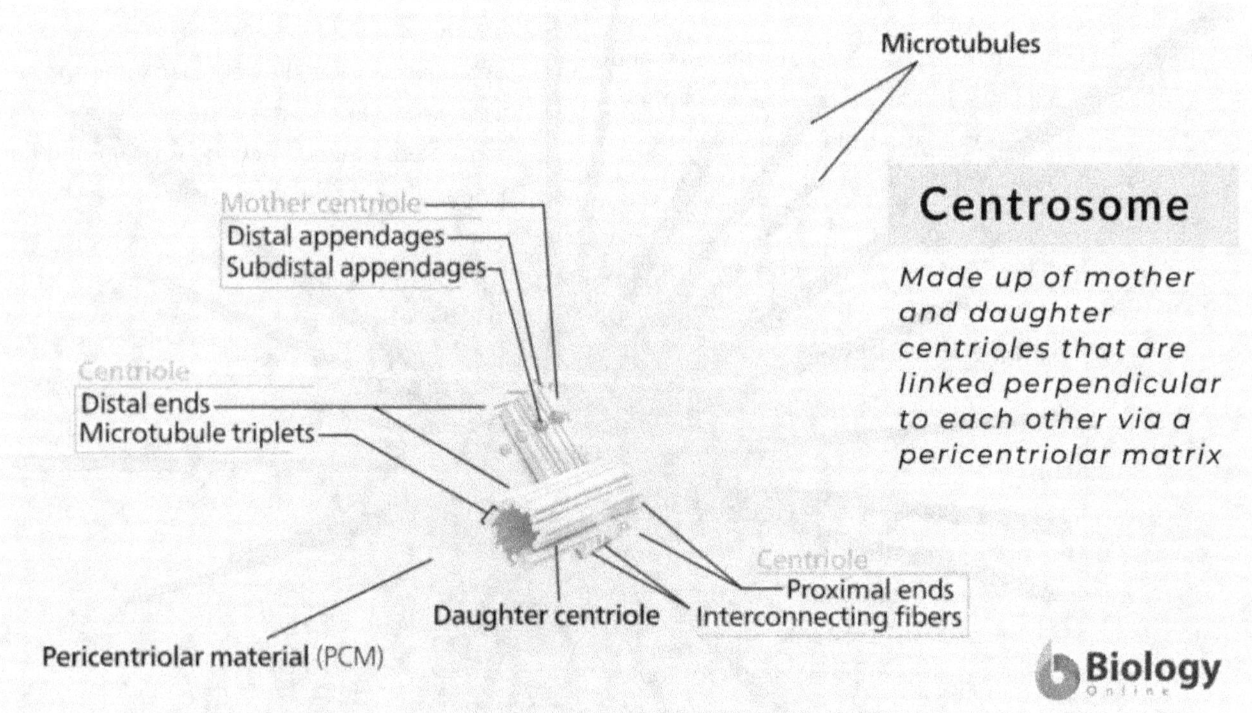

Figure 30: Structure of Centrosome and Centrioles

The similarities and differences between a prokaryotic and a eukaryotic cell have been enlisted in the table below:

Table 5: Comparison of prokaryotic and eukaryotic cell

Characteristic	Prokaryotic Cell	Eukaryotic Cell
Size	Size is usually small ranging between 0.1 µm to 5 µm.	Size is comparatively larger ranging between 5 µm to 100 µm.
Nucleus	The organized nucleus is absent. A nucleoid is found instead.	An organized nucleus is found which contains a nuclear envelope, chromatin, nucleoli, and nucleoplasm.
Histone Proteins	DNA is not associated with histone proteins i.e., Naked	Nuclear DNA is associated with histone proteins.
Location of DNA	DNA lies freely in the cytoplasm. It is not associated with any organelle.	Most of the DNA is nuclear i.e., lies within the nucleus. The rest of the DNA lies in the mitochondria and plastids.
Shape of DNA	Usually, circular DNA is found.	Nuclear DNA is linear, extra DNA is circular.
Plasmids	Small, circular, self-replicating, extranuclear DNA called **plasmids** are present.	Plasmids are absent.
Cell wall composition	Contains muramic acid.	The cell wall is absent in animal cells. Other eukaryotic cells, it does not contain muramic acid.
Other cell organelles	ER, mitochondria, Golgi Apparatus, lysosomes, and centrioles are absent.	ER, mitochondria, Golgi apparatus, and lysosomes are present. Centrioles are usually present in animal cells.
Ribosomes	70S ribosomes are present.	80S ribosomes are present. 70S ribosomes are present only in plastids and mitochondria.
Mesosome	Mesosome is present as an infolding of the cell membrane.	Mesosome is absent.
Flagella structure	Single-stranded flagella present without differentiation of axoneme and sheath.	9+2 array i.e., 11 strands are found. Differentiation into axoneme and sheath is shown.
Transcription	Take place in the cytoplasm.	Takes place in the nucleus.

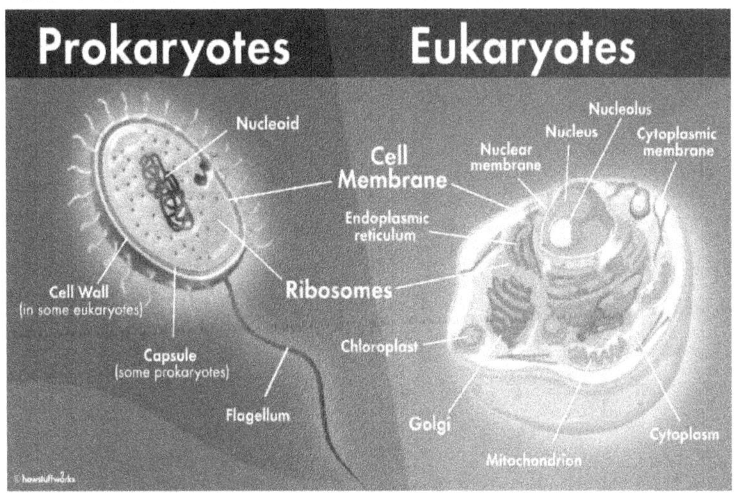

General similarities and differences between a plant cell and an animal cell have been enlisted in the table below:

Table 6: Comparison of plant cell and animal cell

Characteristic	Plant Cell	Animal Cell
Cell Wall	Present	Absent
Plastids	Present	Absent
Centrioles	Present only in lower plants	Present in all animal cells
Vacuoles	Contains a large central vacuole	Many small vacuoles are present
Nucleus	Lies in the periphery	Lies in the center
Cilia	Usually, absent	Present
Lysosome	Rare	Present
Spindle	Anastral (no centrioles and asters)	Amphiastral (presence of two asters)
Reserve food	Starch and fat	Glycogen and fat
Cellular connection	Through plasmodesmata of cell wall	Through junctions

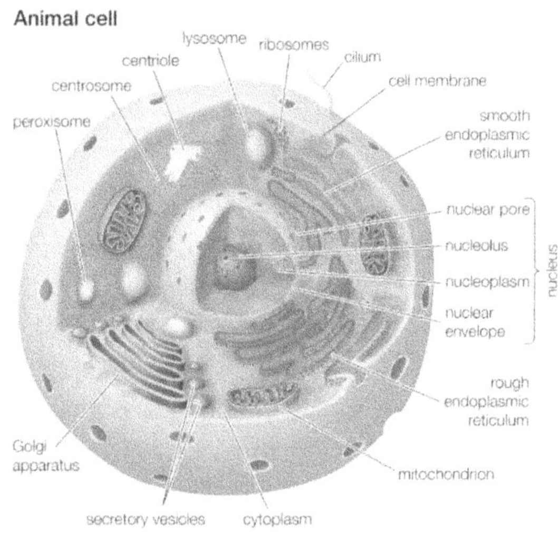

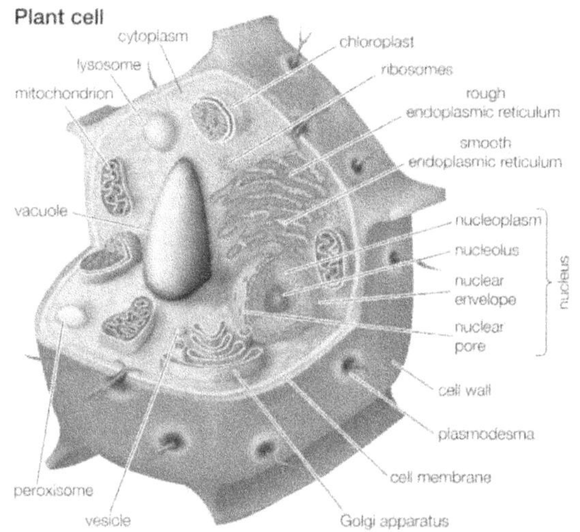

Supplementary Knowledge 

Idioblast

➢ An idioblast is a plant cell that differs from its neighboring cells. They contain cell inclusions for the storage of reserves, excretory materials, pigments, and minerals.

Cellular totipotency in plants cells

➢ Cellular totipotency is the ability to form a complete plant from a single cell. Plant cells show totipotency i.e., a single plant cell can divide and produce all of the differentiated cells.

Tools and Techniques used in Biology

➢ The following tools and techniques play a very important role in the study of the internal structures of a cell:

(1) Microscopy

- A microscope is an instrument used to view objects which naked eyes cannot see.
- Anton van Leeuwenhoek discovered the microscope and therefore he is known as the **father of microscopy.**
- Microscope can be broadly categorized into light microscope and electron microscope.
- In a light microscope glass lenses are used to focus light for image formation.
- The minimum cell size viewed under a

microscope is 0.25 µm.

- An electron microscope uses a beam of electrons instead of light.
- The magnifying power of a microscope is defined as the ratio of the magnified image formed by the microscope to that formed in the retina of a normal unaided eye.
- Resolving power is the ability to differentiate two points as distinct and separate.
- The resolving power of a compound microscope is a 3000Å.
- The different types of microscopes are discussed below:

I. Light microscope

- ❖ **Compound microscope (or bright field microscope)**
  - Light is used for illumination.
  - Two lenses are used in a combination known as condenser and objective.
  - Specimen is seen against a bright background.
  - Stained specimens can be observed.
- ❖ **Dark field microscope**
  - The specimen appears bright against a dark background.
  - Used for viewing live microorganisms.
- ❖ **Phase-contrast microscope**
  - Invented by Fritz-Zernike.
  - Staining of the specimen is not required.
  - Internal structure of living specimens can be observed.
- ❖ **Fluorescence microscope**
  - Fluorescent dyes e.g., acridine orange is used for staining.
  - Fluorescent microbes emit light.
  - Used for rapid identification of microbes in clinical specimens.
- ❖ **Confocal microscope**
  - Laser light is used for illuminating one plane of the specimen at a time.
  - Two and three-dimensional can be obtained.

II. Electron microscope

- ❖ **Transmission electron microscope**
  - Developed by Knoll and Ruska.
  - The beam of electrons passes through the specimen.
  - Two-dimensional images are produced.
  - Structures smaller than 0.2 m can also be resolved.
  - Viruses and ultrastructure of cellular parts can be observed.
- ❖ **Scanning electron microscope**
  - Discovered by Marvin Minsky.
  - Electrons are reflected from the specimen.
  - Three-dimensional images are produced.

(2) Cell fractionation

- Cell fractionation is the process of separating subcellular components after rupturing the cells.
- It helps in studying structural and functional properties of cellular constituents.
- It involves the following steps:
  - ❖ **Homogenization**
    - Cells are ruptured to release their constituents.
    - cells are ruptured using methods like high pressure, sonification, osmotic shock, etc.
  - ❖ **Centrifugation**
    - The various components of the homogenate are separated by applying increased centrifugal force.

- The constituents are separated based on density, shape, and size.
- The rate at which different components separate is described in terms of sedimentation coefficient or Svedberg unit.
- The steps of centrifugation are:

  (i) Differential velocity centrifugation:
  Subcellular organelles are separated based on differences in their size.

  (ii) Equilibrium density gradient centrifugation:
  The organelle fractions obtained after differential velocity centrifugation are used to separate and purify organelles based on their densities. Cesium chloride (CsCl) is used for this process.

(3) Chromatography

- It was invented by Michael Tswett.
- Cellular constituents are separated based on the partition coefficient.
- Each component moves differently through a stationary medium under the influence of a moving solvent.
- It is used for the isolation and purification of various substances e.g., pigments, amino acids, etc.
- The various types of chromatography are column chromatography, partition chromatography, gas chromatography, affinity chromatography, ion-exchange chromatography, and gel filtration chromatography.

(4) Cytological staining

- Stains are dyes that are used to impart a colour to specimens to make them visible under a microscope.
- Stains used to colour for highlighting and viewing individual components:
  - Acetocarmine-Chromosome
  - Eosin-Cytoplasm
  - Ruthenium-Proteins
  - Janus green B-Mitochondria
  - Neutral red-Plant vacuoles

(5) Spectrophotometry

- Used for estimating the quantity of protein and nucleic acids in solution.
- The principle employed is the absorption of light at a different wavelength.

(6) Electrophoresis

- Molecules are separated from a mixture by applying an electric field.
- They are separated based on the charge/mass ratio.
- Examples-PAGE (polyacrylamide gel electrophoresis) is used for separating proteins.

(7) Autoradiography

- Radioactive isotopes called tracers are used in this technique.
- It is useful for studying the functions of organelles, DNA replication, transcription, translation, and metabolic pathways.

(8) Flow cytometry

- Cells are suspended in a fluid and made to pass through electron detection apparatus.
- This technique is used for the counting and identification of cells and chromosomes.

(9) X-ray crystallography

- Used for determining the arrangement of atoms in a molecule.

From AIPMT, NEET, and Other Competition Exams

1. **The basic unit of life is:**
   (a) Cell
   (b) Tissue
   (c) Organ
   (d) Organ system

2. **The study of cellular structure and function is called:**
   (a) Morphology
   (b) Cytology
   (c) Anatomy
   (d) Microbiology

3. **Honeycomb structure in cork was first observed by:**
   (a) Robert Hooke
   (b) Leeuwenhoek
   (c) Altmann and Kolliker
   (d) Schleiden and Schwann

4. **The cells discovered in a thin section of cork were actually:**
   (a) Cell walls   (b) Cellulose
   (c) Protoplasm   (d) Nuclei

5. **Robert Hooke coined the term cell in:**   **(BHU 2008)**
   (a) 1650   (b) 1665
   (c) 1865   (d) 1890

6. **The Father of cytology is:**
   (a) Theodore Schwann
   (b) Robert Hooke
   (c) Rudolf Virchow
   (d) Anton van Leeuwenhoek

7. **Who first saw and describe a live cell?**   **(HPPMT 2010)**
   (a) Rudolf Virchow
   (b) Theodore Schwann
   (c) Anton van Leeuwenhoek
   (d) Mathias Schleiden

8. **Cell theory was first proposed in:**
   (a) 1836-37   (b) 1838-39
   (c) 1838-39   (d) 1665-66

9. **Which of the statement is correct?**
   (a) All organisms have only one cell.
   (b) All organisms comprise a basic unit called a cell.
   (c) Cell theory is given by Rudolf Virchow.
   (d) Robert Hooke discovered the nucleus.

10. **The invention of which of the following enabled the study of structural details of a cell:**
    (a) Telescope
    (b) Electron microscope
    (c) Centrifuge
    (d) None of the above

11. **Schleiden and Schwann proposed:**
    (a) Brownian movement
    (b) Cell Theory
    (c) Protoplasm as the physical basis of life
    (d) None of the above

12. **According to cell theory:**
    (a) Cells are the fundamental structural units of organisms
    (b) Cell reproduces
    (c) Cells are living
    (d) Cell has nuclei

13. **What is the size of microtubules?**   **(HPPMT 2010)**
    (a) 25 nm
    (b) 10 nm
    (c) 7 nm
    (d) 15 nm

14. **The largest isolated single cell is:**
    (a) Egg of Ostrich
    (b) Nerve Cell
    (c) Sclerenchyma fiber
    (d) None of the above

15. **Cell theory was propounded by:**   **(AIIMS 2011)**
    (a) A botanist
    (b) A zoologist
    (c) Both (a) and (b)
    (d) A psychologist

16. **Living beings are made up of cells. This was first stated by:**
    (a) Lamarck
    (b) Von Helmont
    (c) Schleiden and Schwann
    (d) Hugo de Vries

17. **The cell as a basic unit of structure of living things was discovered by:**
    (a) Schleiden and Schwann
    (b) Mendel
    (c) Robert Hooke
    (d) Aristotle

18. **In 1831, Robert Brown discovered:**   **(Odisha 2007)**
    (a) Cell   (b) Dictyosome
    (c) Nucleus   (d) Nucleolus

19. **Father of cytology is:**
    (a) Schleiden
    (b) Anton van Leeuwenhoek
    (c) Robert Hooke
    (d) Robert Brown

20. **New cells generate from:**   **(HPPMT 2010)**
    (a) Bacterial fermentation

(b) Regeneration of old cell

(c) Pre-existing cell

(d) Abiotic cell

21. The smallest known cell is that of:

(a) PPLO

(b) *Volvox*

(c) Paramecium

(d) RBC

22. Cell theory states that:

(a) All cells are living

(b) All cells have the nucleus

(c) Cells are fundamental structural and functional units of living organism

(d) Cell reproduce by mitosis and meiosis

23. Omnis cellula-e-cellula is a generalization given by:

(RPMT 2011)

(a) Lamarck

(b) Dutrochet

(c) Leeuwenhoek

(d) Virchow

24. Schwann and Schleiden formulated the cell theory by studying different types of:

(a) Plants and animals respectively

(b) Animals and plants respectively

(c) Only plants

(d) Only animals

25. Who proposed cell lineage/cell always arises from pre-existing cells?

(a) Lamarck   (b) Virchow

(c) Schwann   (d) Darwin

26. In which year did Rudolf Virchow explain how new cells arise?

(a) 1850   (b) 1855

(c) 1860   (d) 1865

27. Ultrastructure of the cell can be observed through:

(MPPMT 2013)

(a) Simple microscope

(b) Light microscope

(c) Phase contrast microscope

(d) Electron microscope

28. Longest plant cell is:

(a) Xylem fiber

(b) Parenchyma

(c) Sclerenchyma fiber

(d) Collenchyma

29. Which is not a statement from the cell theory?

(a) All cells arise from pre-existing cells

(b) Cells can be divided into prokaryotic and eukaryotic cell

(c) All living organisms are composed of cells and their products

(d) Cells are the structural and functional units of life

30. Longest cell in the human body is:

(a) Bone cell

(b) Nerve cell

(c) Leg muscle cell

(d) Heart muscle cell

31. Which of the following cells is biconcave?

(a) RBC   (b) WBC

(c) Platelets   (d) Nerve cell

32. Choose the statement which is incorrect about prokaryotic cells:

(a) Prokaryotic cells are smaller than eukaryotic cells

(b) Prokaryotic cells multiply more rapidly

(c) Prokaryotic cells show more variation

(d) Prokaryotic cells have both nucleus and membrane-bound organelles

33. Choose the correct option:

(a) Spherical-shaped – Bacillus

(b) Rod-shaped – Vibrio

(c) Comma-shaped – Coccus

(d) spiral-shaped - Spirillum

34. Which of the following do not possess a cell wall?

(a) Mycoplasma   (b) *Pinus*

(c) *E. coli*   (d) *Spirogyra*

35. Which of the following is seen only in a prokaryotic cell?

(a) Dictyosome

(b) Ribosome

(c) Mesosome

(d) Endoplasmic reticulum

36. Which structures perform the function of mitochondria in bacteria?

(a) Cell wall

(b) Mesosome

(c) Nucleoid

(d) Ribosome

37. Extension of the plasma membrane in a prokaryotic cell is:

(a) Mesosome

(b) Hopanoid

(c) Ribosome

(d) None of these

38. What is genophore?

(a) DNA in prokaryotes

(b) DNA and RNA in prokaryotes

(c) DNA and protein in prokaryotes

(d) RNA in prokaryotes

39. Which of the following structure is not found in prokaryotic cells?

(a) Plasma membrane

(b) Nuclear membrane

(c) Ribosome

(d) Mesosome

40. The infoldings of mesosomes are in the form of:

(a) Vesicles

(b) Tubules

(c) Lamellae

(d) All of the above

41. **What is the function of inclusion bodies?**

(a) Storage

(b) Respiration

(c) Digestion

(d) Locomotion

42. **Choose the incorrect statement:**

(a) Gram-positive bacteria have a thick cell wall containing many layers of peptidoglycan and teichoic acid

(b) Gram-negative bacteria have a thin cell wall with only a few layers of peptidoglycan

(c) Gram-positive and gram-negative bacteria differ in the structure of their cell envelope

(d) Gram-positive bacteria are surrounded by another lipid the membrane containing lipo-polysaccharides and lipoproteins

43. **Teichoic acid occurs in the wall of:**

(a) Gram-positive bacteria

(b) Gram-negative bacteria

(c) Mycoplasma

(d) Plasma membrane

44. **Pigment containing membranous extensions found in prokaryotic cells are called:**

(a) Flagella

(b) Mesosome

(c) Chromatophores

(d) Pili

45. **Which of the following help in locomotion in prokaryotes?**

(a) Pili

(b) Flagella

(c) Mesosome

(d) Fimbriae

46. **Cell wall shows:**

(a) Complete permeability

(b) Semi permeability

(c) Different permeability

(d) Impermeability

47. **Outermost layer of cell wall:**

(a) Plasmalemma

(b) Secondary wall

(c) Middle lamella

(d) Primary wall

48. **The longest portion of the flagella is the:**

(a) Basal body

(b) Hook

(c) Filament

(d) None of the these

49. **Choose the function of pili:**

(a) Locomotion

(b) Respiration

(c) Adhesion to rocks and host tissue

(d) Attachment to the recipient cell

50. **Choose the function of Fimbriae:**

(a) Locomotion

(b) Respiration

(c) Adhesion to rocks and host tissue

(d) Attachment to the recipient cell

51. **Which one occurs in both prokaryotic and plant cells?**

(a) Nucleus

(b) Chloroplast

(c) Cell wall

(d) Mitochondria

52. **Which one of the following organisms is not an example of a eukaryotic cell?**

(a) *Escherichia coli*

(b) *Euglena viridis*

(c) *Amoeba proteus*

(d) *Paramecium caudatum*

53. **Cell organelle present in both prokaryotic and eukaryotic cells:**

(a) Ribosome

(b) E. R

(c) Mitochondria

(d) Nucleus

54. **Prokaryotic ribosomes are:**

(a) 50S (b) 60S

(c) 70S (d) 80S

55. **The cell theory is not applicable on:**

(a) Algae (b) Fungi

(c) Lichens (d) Viruses

56. **Prokaryotic cell does not possess:**

(a) Chromosome

(b) Ribosome

(c) Mitochondria

(d) Plasma Membrane

57. **Glycocalyx is associated with:**

(a) Plasmalemma

(b) Nucleus

(c) Nucleolus

(d) Nucleosome

58. **Slime layer and capsule are types of which of the following?**

(a) Glycocalyx

(b) Plasmalemma

(c) Cell wall

(d) Cell envelope

59. **Prokaryotic cell wall made up of:**

(a) Peptidoglycan

(b) Hemicellulose

(c) Cellulose

(d) Pectin

60. **Which of the following is similar in both prokaryotic and eukaryotic cells?**

(a) Nucleus

(b) Cell wall

(c) Cell membrane

(d) Mitochondria

61. The three layers of the cell envelope arranged from outer to inner are:

(a) Glycocalyx, plasma membrane, and cell wall

(b) Glycocalyx, cell wall, and plasma membrane

(c) Cell wall, glycocalyx, and plasma membrane

(d) Plasma membrane, glycocalyx, and cell wall

62. Cytoplasm consists of water:

(a) 50%

(b) 60%

(c) 80%

(d) 90%

63. Middle lamella is present:

(a) Inside the secondary wall

(b) Inside the primary wall

(c) Outside the primary wall

(d) In between secondary and tertiary wall

64. Middle lamella represents:

(a) Common wall between adjacent cell

(b) Common membrane covering of two adjacent cells

(c) Pores between adjacent cells

(d) Cementing materials between two adjacent cells

65. An element presents in middle lamella:

(a) Calcium

(b) Potassium

(c) Sodium

(d) Iron

66. Middle lamella is mainly composed of:

(a) Cellulose, and hemicellulose

(b) Calcium pectate and magnesium pectate

(c) Muramic acid

(d) Phosphoglycerides

67. The primary cell wall is made up of:

(a) Lignin and muramic acid

(b) Calcium pectate, and magnesium pectate

(c) Cellulose, hemicellulose, and Glycoproteins

(d) None of the above

68. Secondary wall is found in:

(a) Collenchyma, Sclerenchyma, and xylem vessels

(b) Parenchyma and meristematic cells

(c) Parenchyma, Collenchyma and Sclerenchyma

(d) All plant cells

69. Largest subunit of a prokaryotic ribosome is:

(a) 30S

(b) 40S

(c) 50S

(d) 60S

70. Smaller subunit of a prokaryotic ribosome is:

(a) 10S

(b) 20S

(c) 30S

(d) 40S

71. Polyribosomes are aggregates of:

(a) Ribosomes and rRNA

(b) Only rRNA

(c) RNA and DNA

(d) Several ribosomes held together by a string of mRNA

72. Which of these is an inclusion body?

(a) Phosphate granules

(b) Cyanophycean granules

(c) Glycogen granules

(d) All of the above

73. The term plasmalemma was coined by:

(a) J. Q. Plower

(b) C. Kramer

(c) C. Nageli

(d) Hooke

74. Ribosomes take part in protein synthesis in:

(a) Virus

(b) Prokaryotic cell

(c) Both prokaryotic and eukaryotic cell

(d) Eukaryotic cell

75. Which of these is not true about eukaryotic cells?

(a) All eukaryotic cells are identical

(b) Eukaryotic cells have several membrane bound organelles

(c) Eukaryotic cells have membrane-bound cell organelle

(d) Genetic material of eukaryotic cells are organized into chromosomes

76. Eukaryotic cells differ from prokaryotic cells in possessing:

(a) Chromatin

(b) True Nucleus

(c) Protoplasm

(d) Endoplasmic reticulum

77. The main arena of various activities of a cell is:

(a) Mitochondria

(b) Cytoplasm

(c) Nucleus

(d) Plasma membrane

78. Which of the following is not true about cell walls?

(a) It is non-living

(b) It is a rigid structure

(c) It is the outermost covering of all eukaryotic cells

(d) It was first seen in cork cells by Robert Hooke

79. Cell wall of algae is composed of:

(a) Cellulose, galactans, mannans, and minerals

(b) Cellulose, hemicellulose, pectin, and proteins

(c) Chitin

(d) None of the above

80. **Cell walls of higher plants are composed of:**
    (a) Cellulose, galactans, mannans, and minerals
    (b) Cellulose, hemicellulose, pectin, and proteins
    (c) Chitin
    (d) None of the above

81. **The functions of mesosomes are:**
    (a) Cell wall formation
    (b) DNA replication
    (c) Secretion
    (d) All of the above

82. **The three parts of flagella do not include:**
    (a) Basal Body　　(b) Hook
    (c) Shaft　　(d) Filament

83. **Latest model of the plasma membrane is:**
    (a) Lamellar model
    (b) Unit membrane model
    (c) Fluid mosaic model
    (d) Molecular lipid model

84. **Which of the following is correct about the structure of the plasma membrane?**
    (a) Phospholipids form the main component of lipids
    (b) Proteins are of two types integral and peripheral
    (c) Protein-lipid ratio varies among cells
    (d) All of the above

85. **Fluid mosaic model of the cell membrane was put forward by:**
    (a) Danielli and Davson
    (b) Singer and Nicolson
    (c) Garner and Allard
    (d) Watson and Crick

86. **Fluid mosaic model of plasma membrane proposed that:**
    (a) Upper layer is non-polar and hydrophobic
    (b) Upper layer is polar and hydrophobic
    (c) Phospholipids produce a bilayer in the middle
    (d) Proteins form the middle layer

87. **The plasma membrane consists of:**
    (a) Proteins embedded in a phospholipid bilayer
    (b) Proteins embedded in a polymer of glucose molecules
    (c) Proteins embedded in a carbohydrate bilayer
    (d) Phospholipid embedded in a protein bilayer

88. **Active transport across biomembrane involves:**
    (a) Production of ATP
    (b) Requirement of energy
    (c) Production of toxin
    (d) Release of energy

89. **Which one of the following structures between two adjacent cells is an effective transport pathway?　(AIPMT 2010)**
    (a) Plastoquinone
    (b) Endoplasmic Reticulum
    (c) Plasmalemma
    (d) Plasmodesmata

90. **Plasmodesmata help in:**
    (a) Cytoplasmic streaming
    (b) Synchronous mitotic division
    (c) Locomotion of unicellular organisms
    (d) Movement of substances between cells

91. **Which of the following words cannot be applied to the plasma membrane?**
    (a) Freely permeable
    (b) Elastic
    (c) Delicate
    (d) Living

92. **Detailed study of the plasma membrane was studied after the advent of the electron microscope in:**
    　　　　　　　　　(AMU 2012)
    (a) 1930s
    (b) 1950s
    (c) 1970s
    (d) 1990s

93. **Membrane structure was mostly studied via chemical studies in:**
    (a) RBCs
    (b) WBCs
    (c) Platelets
    (d) Plant cells

94. **Plasma membrane is made up of:**
    (a) Lipid, protein, and water
    (b) Lipid, protein, and manganese
    (c) Lipid carbohydrates
    (d) Lipid, protein, and carbohydrates

95. **Which of the following is an example of active transport across the plasma membrane?**
    (a) Water
    (b) Na^+/K^+ pump
    (c) Neutral Solutes
    (d) None of the above

96. **Which is true about the primary cell wall?**
    (a) It is a thin and elastic layer capable of growth
    (b) Permanent cells have an only a primary cell wall
    (c) As the cell matures, it gradually increases in thickness
    (d) It is present inner to secondary cell wall

97. **Which is true about the position of the secondary wall?**
    (a) Outer to the primary wall and inner to middle lamella

(b) Outer to middle lamella and inner to the primary wall

(c) Outer to the primary wall and inner to the plasma membrane

(d) Outer to the plasma membrane and inner to the primary wall

98. Secondary wall consists of:

(a) Cellulose and hemicellulose

(b) Cellulose, hemicellulose, xylan, and lignin

(c) Calcium pectate and magnesium pectate

(d) Cellulose, hemicellulose, and glycoproteins

99. Which of the following function of the cell wall?

(a) Gives shape of the cell

(b) Protect the cell from mechanical damage

(c) Provides a barrier to undesirable macromolecules

(d) All of the above

100. Plasmodesmata are:

(a) Locomotory structure

(b) Lignified cement between cells

(c) Connection between adjacent cells

(d) Membrane connecting the nucleus and plasmalemma

101. The transfusion diffusion movement in:

(a) Cholesterol movement

(b) Amino acid

(c) Protein

(d) Phospholipid

102. Which of the organelles form the endomembrane system?

(a) Endoplasmic reticulum and Golgi Complex only

(b) Endoplasmic reticulum, mitochondria, and Golgi body

(c) Endoplasmic reticulum, Golgi complex, and lysosomes

(d) Endoplasmic reticulum, Golgi complex, lysosomes, and vacuoles

103. Endoplasmic reticulum first reported by:

(a) Porter, Claude, and Fullam

(b) Danielli and Davson

(c) Singer and Nicolson

(d) Schleiden and Schwann

104. The endoplasmic reticulum remains attached:

(a) Mitochondria

(b) Golgi Body

(c) Nuclear Envelope

(d) Chloroplast

105. Membrane systems are considered to be extensions of the infolded plasma membrane is:

(a) Golgi complex

(b) Plastids

(c) Mitochondria

(d) E. R

106. Which of the following represents the shape of the endoplasmic reticulum?

(a) Cisternae

(b) Tubules

(c) Vesicles

(d) All of the above

107. The surface of the endoplasmic reticulum can be covered with:

(a) Glucose   (b) DNA

(c) RNA   (d) Ribosome

108. RER is well developed in cells engaged in the synthesis of:

(a) Nucleotide

(b) Proteins

(c) Lipids

(d) Secretory products

109. Select the correct statement from the following regarding cell membrane?

(a) Na^+ and K^+ ions move across the cell membrane by passive transport

(b) Proteins make up 60-70% of the cell membrane

(c) Lipids are arranged in a bilayer with polar heads towards the inner part

(d) Fluid mosaic model of the cell membrane was proposed by Singer and Nicolson

110. Diameter of the largest cell (Ostrich's egg) is:

(a) 6 cm

(b) 6 inches

(c) 6 feet

(d) 6 m

111. Active transport is characterized by: **(AMU 2010)**

(a) Require a unique membrane proteins

(b) Highly Selective

(c) Requires ATP

(d) All of the above

112. Transportation across the membrane can be:

(a) Active, passive and facilitated

(b) Only Active

(c) Only Passive

(d) Only Facilitated

113. Plasma membrane help in:

(a) Transport of water only

(b) Osmoregulation

(c) Protein synthesis

(d) Nucleic acid synthesis

114. Carrier proteins are required for which process?

(a) Passive transport

(b) Diffusion

(c) Osmosis

(d) Facilitated transport

115. **Function of the rough endoplasmic reticulum is:**
    (a) Autolysis
    (b) Lipid Synthesis
    (c) Protein synthesis
    (d) Carbohydrate synthesis

116. **Granular ER differs from SER in having:**
    (a) Ribosome on its surface
    (b) No ribosomes
    (c) Both (b) and (c)
    (d) Active role in steroid synthesis

117. **In animal cells, lipid-like steroidal hormones are synthesized in: (MPPMT 2010)**
    (a) R.E.R
    (b) Golgi Bogy
    (c) S.E.R
    (d) Lysosome

118. **The functions of ER include:**
    (a) Protein synthesis
    (b) Lipid synthesis
    (c) Detoxification
    (d) All of these

119. **The difference between RER and SER is that the Rough endoplasmic reticulum:**
                    (NEET 2013)
    (a) Does not contain ribosomes
    (b) Contains ribosome
    (c) Does not transport proteins
    (d) Transport proteins

120. **An interconnected membranous network of the cell composed of vesicles flattened sacs, and tubules are: (KCET 2012)**
    (a) Mitochondria
    (b) E. R
    (c) Lysosomes
    (d) Nucleus

121. **Which is incorrect about the endoplasmic reticulum?**
    (a) It is a network of double membrane-bound tubular structures scattered in the cytoplasm
    (b) It extends from the nucleus to the cell wall, crossing the cytoplasm
    (c) It divides the intracellular space into two distinct compartments
    (d) Ribosomes may or may not be attached to its outer surface

122. **Which of the following is done by the Golgi apparatus?**
    (a) Secretion
    (b) Protein packing
    (c) Transportation of packaged materials
    (d) All of the above

123. **Which of the following is synthesized in the Golgi apparatus?**
    (a) Carbohydrates
    (b) Pigments
    (c) Hormones
    (d) All of the above

124. **Important site for the formation of glycoproteins and glycolipids is: (AIPMT 2011)**
    (a) Lysosome
    (b) Plastids
    (c) Golgi Apparatus
    (d) Vacuole

125. **Golgi apparatus: (DPMT 2011)**
    (a) Modifies and packages proteins
    (b) Occurs in animals
    (c) Found in prokaryotes
    (d) Site for rapid ATP synthesis

126. **Flat membranous bags are characteristic of:**
    (a) Peroxisomes
    (b) Mitochondria
    (c) Lysosomes
    (d) Golgi bodies

127. **Cis and Trans faces are found in:**
    (a) Mitochondria   (b) Chloroplast
    (c) Golgi apparatus (d) Cell wall

128. **Dictyosome is:**
    (a) A single stack of Golgi apparatus found in plants and fungal cells
    (b) Inner membrane of mitochondria
    (c) Stack of thylakoids in chloroplast
    (d) Proteins embedded in the plasma membrane

129. **Select the correct match in the following pairs: (AIPMT 2015)**
    (a) Rough ER – Oxidation of fatty acids
    (b) Smooth ER – Oxidation of phospholipids
    (c) Smooth ER – Synthesis of lipids
    (d) Rough ER – Synthesis of glycogen

130. **Choose the correct combination:**
    (a) Cisternae– Flat, disc-shaped, membrane-bound sacs
    (b) Tubules- Large round structures found on the edges of cis and trans face
    (c) Vesicles- Small, flat structure arising from the periphery of the cisternae
    (d) None of the above is correct

131. **Cell organelle connected with intracellular digestion of macromolecule is:**
                    (Kerala 2009)
    (a) Lysosome
    (b) Peroxisome
    (c) Polysome
    (d) Glyoxysomes

132. **The discoverer of the lysosome is:**
   (a) Palade   (b) de Duve
   (c) Porter   (d) Golgi

133. **The lysosome is known as a suicidal bag of cells because they have:**
   (a) Hydrolytic enzyme
   (b) Parasitic activity
   (c) Food vacuole
   (d) Catabolic enzymes

134. **Lysosomes can digest which of the following?**
   (a) Carbohydrates
   (b) Proteins
   (c) Lipids
   (d) All of these

135. **Functions of the lysosome are:**
   (a) Breakdown of cell substances
   (b) Synthesis of proteins
   (c) Photosynthesis
   (d) Breakdown of water

136. **Lysosomes contain:**
   (a) Carbohydrate
   (b) Hormones
   (c) Nucleic acids
   (d) Hydrolases

137. **Autolysis is connected with:**
   (a) Ribosome
   (b) Kinetosome
   (c) Lysosome
   (d) Golgi apparatus

138. **Lysosomes function in:**
   (a) Extracellular digestion
   (b) Intracellular digestion
   (c) Both (a) and (b)
   (d) Fat breakdown

139. **Lysosome enzymes are active at pH:**
   (a) 5   (b) 7
   (c) 8   (d) Variable

140. **Hydrolytic enzymes of lysosome function at:**
   (a) Acidic pH
   (b) Alkaline pH
   (c) Neutral pH
   (d) Both (b) and (c)

141. **Lysosomes are called as they have:**
   (a) Oxidizing enzymes
   (b) Digestive enzymes
   (c) Respiratory enzymes
   (d) Carboxylation enzymes

142. **What would happen if lysosomes get ruptured in a cell?**
   (a) Cell dies
   (b) Cell shrinks
   (c) Cell swells up
   (d) Nothing would happen

143. **Lysosomes are formed from:**
   (BHU 2007)
   (a) E.R
   (b) Golgi bodies
   (c) Mitochondria
   (d) Both (a) and (b)

144. **Intracellular digestion occurs through:**
   (a) Autophagy
   (b) Heterophagy
   (c) Both (a) and (b)
   (d) None of these

145. **The vacuole is covered by a membrane called:**
   (a) Tonoplast
   (b) Plasmalemma
   (c) Cell membrane
   (d) Cell wall

146. **Which is not a function of the vacuole in a plant cell?**
   (a) Storage
   (b) Waste disposal
   (c) Production of H_2O_2
   (d) Cell elongation and protection

147. **Major function is contractile vacuole is?**
   (a) Excretion
   (b) Storage
   (c) Osmoregulation
   (d) Circulation

148. **That one located inside a vacuole is:**
   (a) Tonoplast
   (b) Matrix
   (c) Ergastic substances
   (d) Cell Sap

149. **Cell vacuole contains:**
   (a) Water
   (b) Metabolic gases
   (c) Water and dissolved substances
   (d) Cytoplasm

150. **In a plant cell, the vacuole:**
   (AIPMT 2008
   (a) Contains air and lacks membrane
   (b) Contains water and excretory materials but lack membrane
   (c) Contains storage protein and lipid
   (d) Contains water and excretory substances

151. **Which is correctly matched?**
   (a) Sap vacuole- Found in green bacterial cells
   (b) Contractile vacuole- Helps in osmoregulation and excretion *e.g. Amoeba*
   (c) Food vacuole- Contains dissolved salts and maintains turgor pressure in plant cells
   (d) Gas vacuole- Formed by engulfing food particles *e.g.* protists.

152. **Functions of vacuole:**
   (a) Storage of substances including waste products of a

(b) In plant cells the tonoplast helps in the transfer of ions and other materials against the concentration gradient into the vacuole

(c) Contribute to osmotic properties of cells

(d) All of these

153. The organelles called the powerhouse of the cell is:

(a) Chloroplast

(b) Mitochondria

(c) Golgi Bogy

(d) Nucleoli

154. Who discovered mitochondria?

(a) Richard Altman

(b) Christian de Duve

(c) Camillo Golgi

(d) C. Benda

155. The term mitochondria was coined by:

(a) Kolliker

(b) Benda

(c) Flemming

(d) Altman

156. Folding of the inner mitochondrial membrane is called:

(a) Grana

(b) Thylakoids

(c) Cristae

(d) $F_0 - F_1$ structures

157. Mitochondrial cristae are sites of:

(a) Breakdown of macromolecules

(b) Protein synthesis

(c) Phosphorylation of flavoproteins

(d) Redox reaction

158. Which is incorrect about mitochondria?

(a) Mitochondria divided by binary fission

(b) Mitochondria contain their own linear DNA

(c) Mitochondria are abundant in actively metabolizing cells and tissues

(d) Mitochondria are sites of aerobic respiration

159. Energy releasing reactions in a cell occur in:

(a) Cell wall

(b) Ribosomes

(c) Mitochondria

(d) Plastids

160. Which of the following cell organelles is responsible for extracting energy from carbohydrates to form ATP?

(NEET 2017)

(a) Ribosomes   (b) Chloroplast

(c) Mitochondrion   (d) Lysosome

161. Oxidative electron transport occurs in:

(a) Chloroplast

(b) Outer membrane of mitochondria

(c) Cristae

(d) E.R

162. The inner compartment of mitochondria is called:

(a) Cristae

(b) Matrix

(c) Both (a) and (b)

(d) None of these

163. Mitochondria are sites of:

(a) Calvin cycle

(b) Krebs cycle

(c) Hill reaction

(d) Glycolysis

164. Mitochondria are semi-autonomous as they possess:

(a) DNA

(b) DNA+RNA

(c) DNA + RNA + Ribosomes

(d) Proteins

165. Respiratory enzyme occurs in:

(WB 2009)

(a) Chloroplast

(b) Mitochondria

(c) Lysosome

(d) Peroxisomes

166. The size of mitochondria in the plant cell is:

(a) 3 – 4 µm long

(b) 2 – 4 µm long

(c) 1 – 4 µm long

(d) 0.1 – 1 µm long

167. Which is the correct statement?

(AMU 2010)

(a) Cristae are the sites of the electron transport chain

(b) Mitochondrial matrix is the site of Krebs cycle

(c) Both (a) and (b)

(d) None of the above

168. The term plastid was coined by:

(a) Haeckel   (b) Strasburger

(c) Virchow   (d) Flemmi

169. Plastids are absent in:

(a) Lower plants

(b) Higher plants

(c) Euglenoids

(d) Animals

170. Which is not a plastid?

(DPMT 2008)

(a) Chloroplast

(b) Mitoplast

(c) Chromoplast

(d) Leucoplast

171. The colour of chromoplast can be:

(a) Yellow

(b) Red

(c) Orange

(d) All of the above

172. Orange-yellow colors of flowers and fruits are due to:

(a) Chloroplast

(b) Leucoplast

(c) Aleuroplast

(d) Chromoplast

173. Amyloplasts are connected with the storage of:

(a) Starch

(b) Fat

(c) Glycogen

(d) Protein

174. Protein storing plastids are:

(a) Amyloplast

(b) Elaioplast

(c) Aleuroplast

(d) Chromoplast

175. Fat storing plastids are:

(a) Amyloplast

(b) Aleuroplast

(c) Elaioplast

(d) All of these

176. Who coined the term chloroplast?

(a) Haeckel

(b) Sachimpor

(c) Virchow

(d) Flemming

177. The shape of chloroplast in the higher plant is:

(a) Discoid

(b) Girdle shaped

(c) Reticulate

(d) Cup-shaped

178. The average number of chloroplasts in mesophyll cells of green plants is:

(a) 5 – 10

(b) 100 – 200

(c) 20 – 40

(d) 50 – 60

179. The space limited by the inner membrane of a chloroplast is called:

(a) Grana

(b) Thylakoid

(c) Stroma

(d) Stomatal lamellae

180. A flat disc-like structure present in the chloroplast is:

(a) Stroma

(b) Thylakoid

(c) Loculus

(d) Margin

181. Number of membranes separating intra thylakoid space from the cytoplasm is:

(a) 4   (b) 3

(c) 2   (d) 1

182. The structures that are formed by stacking of organized flattened membranous sacs in the chloroplasts are:

(a) Stroma

(b) Cristae

(c) Grana

(d) Stroma lamellae

183. In chloroplasts the chlorophyll is located in:

(AIPMT 2005)

(a) Stroma

(b) Grana

(c) Pyrenoid

(d) Both (a) and (b)

184. Chlorophyll occurs in chloroplast:

(a) Inner membrane

(b) Thylakoid membrane

(c) Outer membrane

(d) Stroma

185. The thylakoid of different grana is connected by flat membranous

tubules called:

(a) Stroma lamellae

(b) Inter grana

(c) Both (a) and (b)

(d) None of the above

186. The space enclosed by the thylakoid membrane is called:

(a) Lumen   (b) Lamella

(c) Stroma   (d) Inter grana

187. Chloroplast is self-replicating units as they possess:

(a) DNA

(b) RNA

(c) Neither DNA nor RNA

(d) Both DNA and RNA

188. Circular DNA is collated in:

(a) Stroma

(b) Grana

(c) Inter grana

(d) Lumen

189. Factors of synthesis of sugar in autotrophic eukaryotes are:

(a) Chloroplast

(b) Mitochondria

(c) E. R

(d) Ribosome

190. Which of the following function does chloroplast perform?

(a) Photosynthesis

(b) Respiration

(c) Storage of food

(d) None of these

191. Ribosomes of bacterial mitochondria and chloroplast are of:

(a) 50S   (b) 80S

(c) 70S   (d) 30S

192. Ribosomes were discovered under E.M by:

(a) Golgi   (b) Porter

(c) De Robertis   (d) Pallade

193. **What is true for ribosome:**
    (AIPMT 2012)
    (a) Prokaryotic ribosomes are the 80S
    (b) Composed of RNA and protein
    (c) Found only in eukaryotic cells
    (d) They are self-splicing introns of some RNAs

194. **70S ribosomes are found in:**
    (a) Eukaryotic cell
    (b) Prokaryotic cell
    (c) Mitochondria
    (d) Both (b) and (c)

195. **Eukaryotic ribosomes are:**
    (a) 30S
    (b) 50S
    (c) 70S
    (d) 80S

196. **Ribosomes are granules made of:**
    (a) rRNA and tRNA
    (b) mRNA and tRNA
    (c) rRNA and proteins
    (d) mRNA and proteins

197. **Subunits of 80S ribosomes are:**
    (DUMET 2008)
    (a) 40S
    (b) 60S
    (c) Both (a) and (b)
    (d) None of these

198. **Subunits of 70s ribosomes are:**
    (a) 30S and 50S
    (b) 30s and 40S
    (c) 35S and 35S
    (d) 20S and 50S

199. **Which is true about ribosomes?**
    (a) They are negatively charged
    (b) They are membrane-bound
    (c) Mg^{2+} is necessary for the binding of the two subunits
    (d) None of the above

200. **The suffix 'S' in the ribosome unit indicates:**
    (a) Sedimentation coefficient
    (b) Solubility
    (c) Surface area
    (d) Size

201. **'S' in 70S is:**
    (a) Svedberg's unit
    (b) Solubility
    (c) Surface Area
    (d) Size

202. **Ribosomes are classified as per:**
    (a) Size
    (b) Volume
    (c) Sedimentation rate
    (d) Weight

203. **Ribosomes bound to membranes synthesis:**
    (a) Secretory protein
    (b) Integral membrane protein
    (c) Lysosomal proteins
    (d) All of the above

204. **Free ribosome synthesizes:**
    (a) Soluble cytoplasmic proteins
    (b) Peripheral membrane proteins
    (c) Mitochondrial proteins
    (d) All of the above

205. **Peptidyl transferase is found within:**
    (a) Larger subunits
    (b) Smaller subunits
    (c) Both (a) and (b)
    (d) None of the above

206. **The cytoskeleton is formed of:**
    (a) Callose deposit
    (b) Cellulose microfibrils
    (c) Calcium carbonate granules
    (d) Proteinaceous filaments

207. **The cytoskeleton is made up of:**
    (a) Microtubules and E.R
    (b) Microtubules and microfilaments
    (c) Cytoplasm
    (d) Cytoplasm with a network of microtubules and microfilaments

208. **Microtubules are made up of:**
    (a) Actin
    (b) Keratin
    (c) Tubulin
    (d) Dynein

209. **Choose the correct combination:**
    (a) Intermediate filaments - Acidic protein
    (b) Microtubules-Actin
    (c) Microfilament- Tubulin
    (d) Intermediate filaments-Tubulin

210. **Microtubules take part in:**
    (a) Formation of spindle fibers
    (b) Movement of cilia and flagella
    (c) Both (a) and (b)
    (d) Cyclosis

211. **Choose the function of the cytoskeleton:**
    (a) Provides mechanical support to the cell
    (b) Maintains the shape of a cell
    (c) Helps in the formation of spindle fibers
    (d) All of the above

212. **Flagella occur in:**   **(WB 2007)**
    (a) Eukaryotic cell
    (b) Prokaryotic cell
    (c) Viruses
    (d) Both (a) and (b)

213. **The core of cilia and flagella is known as:**
    (a) Axoneme
    (b) Actin
    (c) Axis
    (d) Acrosome

214. **Arrangement of ciliary microtubules is:**
    (a) 9 + 2
    (b) 9 + 4
    (c) 9 + 3
    (d) 9 + 9

215. **The number of microtubules in a flagellum including those sharing three protofilaments is:**

(CPMT 2010)

(a) 10

(b) 11

(c) 20

(d) 22

216. **Axonemal arrangement of microtubules is: (AMU 2012)**

(a) 6 peripheral pairs of doublets and one central pair of singlets

(b) 6 peripheral pairs of doublets and one central singlet

(c) 9 peripheral pairs of doublets and one pair of central singlets

(d) 9 peripheral pairs of doublets and one central singlet

217. **Which of the following statement about cilia is not correct?**

(a) Organized beating of cilia is controlled by fluxes of Ca2+ across the membrane

(b) Cilia are hair-like cellular appendages

(c) Cilia contain an outer ring of nine doublet microtubules surrounding two singlets

(d) Microtubules of cilia are composed of tubulin

218. **Axoneme with 9+2 microtubular arrangement occurs in:**

(AMU 2009)

(a) Cilia

(b) Flagella

(c) Both (a) and (b)

(d) Centriole

219. **Prokaryotic and eukaryotic flagella differ in:**

(a) Type of movement and placement

(b) Location and mode of functioning

(c) Microtubular structure and function

(d) Microtubular organization and type of movement

220. **Cilia are:**

(a) Short, 5-10 μm

(b) Numerous

(c) with weeping and pendular movement

(d) All of the above

221. **Who introduced the term centrosome?**

(a) Plower

(b) de Duve

(c) Lamarck

(d) Boveri

222. **Centrioles and centrosomes occur in the cells of:**

(a) Green plants

(b) Animals

(c) Bacteria and cyanobacteria

(d) Both (b) and (c)

223. **The centrosome is absent in:**

(a) Cells in higher plants

(b) Cells in lower plants

(c) Cells of higher animals

(d) Cells of lower animals

224. **Which one is without an external covering?**

(a) Lysosome

(b) Golgi Apparatus

(c) Centrosome

(d) Centriole

225. **How many centrioles does a centrosome have?**

(a) 2

(b) 3

(c) 4

(d) 1

226. **What is false about diplosomes?**

(a) They are formed on 2 centrioles

(b) They lie parallel to each other

(c) Each centriole has a cartwheel like organization

(d) Each centriole has two regions – central and peripheral

227. **The centrioles are surrounded by:**

(a) Pericentriolar materials

(b) Nuclear materials

(c) Double membrane

(d) None of the above

228. **Organelle important in spindle formation during nuclear division is: (JKCMEE 2005)**

(a) Centriole

(b) Golgi body

(c) Chloroplast

(d) Mitochondria

229. **Aster formation is related to:**

(a) Centriole

(b) Mitochondria

(c) Chloroplast

(d) Nucleus

230. **The name chromatin was coined by: (Kerala 2010)**

(a) Robert Brown

(b) Flemming

(c) Camillo Golgi

(d) Rudolf Virchow

231. **Which of the following is multinucleate?**

(a) RBCs

(b) Osteoclasts

(c) Platelets

(d) Nerve Cells

232. **Which is enucleate?**

(a) RBCs

(b) Sieve tube cells

(c) Both (a) and (b)

(d) Neither (a) nor (b)

233. **The nucleus is separated from the surrounding cytoplasm by a nuclear membrane which is:**

(a) Single layered with pores

(b) Single layered without pores

(c) Double layered with pores

(d) Double layer without pores

234. **Which is incorrect about the nuclear envelope?**
    (a) It is also called nuclear membrane
    (b) It consists of two parallel membranes
    (c) The space between the two membranes are called perinuclear space
    (d) None of the above

235. **The outer nuclear membrane is continuous with the:**
    (a) Mitochondria
    (b) E. R
    (c) Cell membrane
    (d) Vacuole

236. **Do these nuclear pores help in the movement of which of the following?**
    (a) RNA
    (b) Proteins
    (c) Both (a) and (b)
    (d) None of the above

237. **The nucleoplasm contains:**
    (a) Nucleolus
    (b) Chromatin
    (c) Both (a) and (b)
    (d) None of the above

238. **The term nucleolus was coined by:**
    (a) Bowman
    (b) Fontana
    (c) Flemming
    (d) Leeuwenhoek

239. **Which is incorrect about nucleolus?**
    (a) They are spherical structures
    (b) They are membrane-bound
    (c) Cells that are involved in active protein synthesis has a larger and numerous nucleoli

    (d) The nucleolus is the site for active ribosomal RNA synthesis

240. **A conspicuous rounded body present in the nucleoplasm and attached to a particular chromosome at the definite place is:**   (AIIMS)
    (a) Plasmid
    (b) Karyolymph
    (c) Nucleolus
    (d) E. R

241. **An outer covering membrane is absent over:**
    (a) Nucleolus
    (b) Lysosome
    (c) Mitochondrion
    (d) Plastid

242. **rRNA is actively synthesized in:**
    (a) Lysosomes
    (b) Nucleolus
    (c) Nucleoplasm
    (d) Ribosomes

243. **Nucleolus is:**
    (a) Rounded structure found in cytoplasm near nucleus
    (b) Rounded structure inside the nucleus and having rRNA
    (c) Rod-shaped structure in cytoplasm near the nucleus
    (d) None of the above

244. **The nucleolus contains which of the following?**
    (a) RNA
    (b) Proteins
    (c) DNA
    (d) All of the above

245. **The total number of chromosomes in a cell human is:**
    (a) 23   (b) 23 pairs
    (c) 46 pairs   (d) 48

246. **Chromosomes are concerned with:**

    (a) Respiration
    (b) Growth
    (c) Transmission of hereditary characters
    (d) Assimilation

247. **Within the nucleus, DNA is organized along with proteins into materials called:**
    (a) Nuclear lamina
    (b) Chromosome
    (c) Chromatid
    (d) Chromatin

248. **Proteins associated with nucleic acid are:**
    (a) Histone
    (b) Globulin
    (c) Albumin
    (d) Scleroprotein

249. **Chromosome consist of:**
                    (MPPMT 2011)
    (a) DNA
    (b) RNA
    (c) Protein
    (d) DNA, RNA, and Protein

250. **DNA occurs in:**
    (a) Mitochondria, plastids, and chromosome
    (b) Chromosome, mitochondria, and ribosomes
    (c) Chromosomes, mitochondria, and cell membrane
    (d) Chromosome, Ribosomes, and cytoplasm

251. **Sister chromatids are joined at:**
    (a) Chromocenter
    (b) Metacenter
    (c) Centromere
    (d) Telomere

252. **Kinetochore is:**
    (a) Granules with centromere
    (b) Disc-shaped structure on the side of centromere

(c) Constriction near chromosome end

(d) End of chromosome

253. Chromosome end is called:

(a) Telomere

(b) Centromere

(c) Satellite

(d) Metamere

254. The shape of the chromosome is:

(a) Centromere

(b) Centrosome

(c) Telomere

(d) Micromere

255. The chromosome that lacks a centromere is:

(a) Acentric

(b) Acrocentric

(c) Metacentric

(d) Telocentric

256. A chromosome with a centromere in the middle is:

(a) Metacentric

(b) Telocentric

(c) Acrocentric

(d) Dicentric

257. Chromosome having terminal centromere capped by telomere is: (HPPMT 2007)

(a) Metacentric

(b) Sub-metacentric

(c) Acrocentric

(d) Telocentric

258. One type of chromosome has a middle centromere whereas the other has a terminal centromere. They are: (Kerala PMT 2015)

(a) Metacentric and acrocentric

(b) Metacentric and telocentric

(c) Sub-metacentric and telocentric

(d) Telocentric and acrocentric

259. A chromosome carrying centromere at one end is:

(a) Acrocentric

(b) Telocentric

(c) Metacentric

(d) Sub-metacentric

260. Chromosomes appearing rod-shaped during anaphase are:

(a) Acrocentric

(b) Metacentric

(c) Telocentric

(d) Sub-metacentric

261. L-shaped chromosomes are:

(a) Sex Chromosomes

(b) Acrocentric

(c) Telocentric

(d) Sub-metacentric

262. A chromosome with a centromere near one end forms shorter and longer arms are: (AMU 2012)

(a) Metacentric

(b) Sub-metacentric

(c) Telocentric

(d) Acrocentric

263. Shape of the metacentric chromosome in anaphase is:

(a) L-shaped   (b) V-shaped

(c) J-shaped   (d) I-shaped

264. Telomeres are:

(a) Initiate RNA synthesis

(b) Help chromatids to move towards poles

(c) Seal ends of chromosomes

(d) Identify correct members of homologous pairs of chromosomes

265. A chromosome having sub terminal centromere is: (AMU 2009)

(a) Acrocentric

(b) Sub-metacentric

(c) type of chromosomes

(d) Metacentric

266. In which chromosome, one arm is very short and one arm very long?   (HPPMT 2012)

(a) Acrocentric

(b) Metacentric

(c) Sub-metacentric

(d) Telocentric

267. Protein synthesis occurs in:

(a) Mitochondria

(b) Chloroplast

(c) Cytoplasm

(d) All of these

268. Plant cell differs from animal cell: (Ch. CET 2012)

(a) Presence of vacuoles

(b) Presence of cell wall and chloroplast

(c) Absence of cell wall

(d) Absence of chloroplast

269. Animal cells do not possess: (MPPMT 2011)

(a) Plasmodesmata

(b) Centrioles

(c) 80S ribosomes

(d) All of these

270. Which one is not a cell inclusion?   (Odisha 2011)

(a) Crystal

(b) Vacuoles

(c) Starch

(d) Fat droplet

271. DNA is not present in: (AIPMT 2015)

(a) Mitochondria

(b) Chloroplast

(c) Ribosomes

(d) Nucleus

272. Double membrane is absent in:

(a) Mitochondria

(b) Chloroplast

(c) Ribosomes

(d) Lysosomes

273. A cell organelle containing hydrolytic enzymes is:

     (NEET II 2016)

(a) Ribosomes

(b) Mesosomes

(c) Lysosome

(d) Microsome

274. rRNA occur in:

     (MHT CET 2008)

(a) Lysosome

(b) Cytosol

(c) Ribosomes

(d) Golgi apparatus

275. All are membrane-bound cell organelles except:

(a) Mitochondria

(b) Lysosome

(c) Sphaerosomes

(d) Ribosomes

276. Which of the following show selectively permeability?

     (Odisha 2005)

(a) Cell membrane

(b) cell wall

(c) Cytoplasm

(d) Protoplasm

277. A single unit membrane surrounds the organelle:

(a) Nucleus

(b) Mitochondrion

(c) Lysosome

(d) Chloroplast

278. A major site for the synthesis of lipids is: **(AIPMT 2014)**

(a) RER

(b) Nucleoplasm

(c) Symplast

(d) SER

279. A semi-autonomous organelle is:

(a) E. R

(b) Lysosome

(c) Peroxisome

(d) Chloroplast

280. Which cell organelle connects the nuclear envelope with the cell membrane?

(a) Lysosome

(b) Golgi body

(c) E. R

(d) Mitochondria

281. Functions of the cell are controlled by:

(a) Protoplasm

(b) Cytoplasm

(c) Nucleolus

(d) Nucleus

282. Which one is not properly paired?

(a) Golgi apparatus	Breaking of complex macromolecules
(b) Endoplasmic reticulum	Protein Synthesis
(c) Mitochondria	Oxidative Phosphorylatio
(d) Chloroplast	Photosynthesis

283. Which cellular part is correctly described? **(AIPMT 2012)**

(a) Thylakoids	Flattened membranous sacs forming grana
(b) Centrioles	Sites for active RNA synthesis
(c) Ribosomes	Those in chloroplasts are larger (80S) while those in cytoplasm are smaller (70S)
(d) Lysosomes	Optimally active at 8.5 pH

284. Which of the following cell organelles is responsible for extracting energy from carbohydrates to form ATP?

     (NEET-2017)

(a) Lysosome

(b) Ribosome

(c) Chloroplast

(d) Mitochondrion

285. Which is the part of the endomembrane system of the eukaryotic cells?

     (JKCMEE 2008)

(a) Mitochondria

(b) Peroxisome

(c) Chloroplast

(d) Golgi bodies

286. Non-Membranous organelle is:

     (RPMT 2011)

(a) Chloroplast

(b) Nucleolus

(c) Centriole

(d) Both (b) and (c)

287. Which organelle is absent in animal cells? **(RPMT 2006)**

(a) Chloroplast

(b) Golgi Apparatus

(c) E. R

(d) Lysosomes

288. Which of the following are not membrane-bound?

     (AIPMT 2015)

(a) Mesosomes

(b) Vacuoles

(c) Ribosomes

(d) Lysosomes

289. From the following statement select, which is true?

     (JKCET 2012)

(a) All cells have a cell wall

(b) Animals cell contain micro tubules but plant cells don't have microtubules

(c) Golgi apparatus is found only in animal cells

(d) Chloroplasts are found in plant cells but not in prokaryotic or animal cells

290. Site of protein synthesis is:

(Chd. CET 2012)

(a) Ribosomes

(b) Nucleus

(c) Mitochondria

(d) DNA

291. Organelle associated with aerobic transpiration is:

(JKCMEE 2005)

(a) Nucleus

(b) Centriole

(c) Chloroplast

(d) Mitochondrion

292. Enzymes connected with the oxidative electron transport system are found in:

(a) Plastids

(b) Mitochondrion

(c) Golgi bodies

(d) E. R

293. Organelles connected with lipid synthesis:

(a) Ribosomes

(b) SER

(c) Golgi body

(d) All of these

294. Higher number of enzymes occur in: **(MPPMT 2007)**

(a) Chloroplast

(b) Peroxisome

(c) Mitochondrion

(d) Lysosome

295. Cellular organelles with membranes are:

(AIPMT 2015)

(a) Lysosome, Golgi apparatus, and mitochondria

(b) Nucleoli, ribosomes, and mitochondria

(c) Chromosomes, ribosomes, and endoplasmic reticulum

(d) Endoplasmic reticulum, ribosomes, and nucleoli

296. The smallest cell organelles are:

(a) Lysosomes

(b) Sphaerosomes

(c) Peroxisomes

(d) Ribosomes

297. Protein synthesis occurs in an animal cell in:

(a) Cytoplasm

(b) Cytoplasm as well as mitochondria

(c) Ribosomes attached to nuclear envelope

(d) Nucleolus as well as cytoplasm

298. Organelle having flattened membrane-bound cisternae and lying near the nucleus is:

(a) Golgi apparatus

(b) Mitochondrion

(c) Centriole

(d) Nucleolus

299. Which one is common amongst nucleus, chloroplast, and mitochondria?

(a) Cristae

(b) Thylakoids

(c) Nucleic acid

(d) Carbohydrates metabolism

300. DNA is present in both:

(AFMC 2011)

(a) Centriole and mitochondria

(b) Ribosomes and plastid

(c) Chloroplasts and mitochondria

(d) Chloroplast and Golgi apparatus

301. Cellular organelles involved in energy transformation are:

(a) Mitochondria and chloroplasts

(b) Chromoplasts and leucoplast

(c) Mitochondria and chromoplasts

(d) Chloroplasts and leucoplasts

302. Out of peroxisomes, lysosomes, and mitochondria a single membrane covering occurs in:

(a) Both peroxisomes and lysosomes

(b) Only peroxisomes

(c) All of the above

(d) None of the above

303. Which one is non-living cell inclusion?

(a) Golgi complex

(b) Centrosome

(c) Vacuole

(d) Ribosome

304. Export house/firm of cell is:

(a) E. R

(b) Golgi body

(c) Nucleus

(d) Lysosome

305. Cell organelle having flattened sac-like cisternae which play a part in packing and secretion is:

(a) Lysosome

(b) Golgi apparatus

(c) Ribosome

(d) Mitochondrion

306. Electron microscope has revealed the presence of:

(a) Ribosomes

(b) Chromosomes

(c) Chloroplast

(d) Leucoplast

307. A plant cell has:

(Odisha 2008)

(a) A large vacuole and rigid cell wall

(b) Centriole for cell division

(c) Centrosome inactive in non-diving cells

(d) Absence of cell membrane

308. **Which is common in plant and animal cells?**

(a) Plastids

(b) Centrioles

(c) Mitochondria

(d) Central vacuole

309. **Plasmids are present in:**

(a) Prokaryotes

(b) Eukaryotes

(c) both (b) and (c)

(d) None of the above

310. **Cell walls of prokaryotes contain:**

(a) Teichoic acid

(b) Lipopolysaccharides

(c) Muramic acid

(d) Cellulose

311. **Starch and fat are reserved food in:**

(a) Plant cell

(b) Animal cell

(c) Both (a) and (b)

(d) None of these

312. **Transcription in prokaryotes takes place in:**

(a) Nucleus

(b) Cytoplasm

(c) Mitochondria

(d) Cell membrane

313. **The cell is not applied for:**

(a) Algae   (b) Fungi

(c) Bacteria   (d) Virus

314. **A cell without a cell wall is termed as:**

(a) Tonoplast   (b) Protoplast

(c) Symplast   (d) Apoplast

315. **Correct sequence of the protein (P) and Lipid (L) in the cell membrane is (as per the lamellae model):**

(a) L – P – L - P

(b) P - L - P – L

(c) P – L – L – P

(d) L – P – P – L

316. **As per the fluid mosaic model, lipids and integral proteins can diffuse randomly. The model has been modified in several aspects. Which of the following statements is incorrect?**

(AIPMT 2005)

(a) Proteins of the cell membrane can travel within the lipid bilayer

(b) Proteins of cell membrane undergo flip-flop movement in lipid bilayer

(c) Protein can remain confined within domains of the membrane

(d) Many proteins remain completely embedded within the lipid bilayer

317. **Which is incorrect about the Golgi apparatus?**

(a) Golgi apparatus was first observed as densely stained reticular structures near the nucleus

(b) The Golgi cisternae are arranged concentrically near the nucleus

(c) The Golgi cisternae have a distinct concave cis or forming face and a convex trans or maturing face

(d) The cis and trans faces are different but interconnected to each other

318. **An elaborate network of filamentous proteinaceous structures which helps in the maintenance of cell shape is called:**   **(RPMT 2011)**

(a) Plasmalemma

(b) Cytoskeleton

(c) Endoplasmic reticulum

(d) Thylakoids

319. **Choose the incorrect statement:**

(a) Cilia and flagella are thin hair like outgrowths extending from the cell membrane

(b) The structure and function of both cilia and flagella are similar

(c) They can distinguish on the basis of their size and number

(d) Flagella are longer and more in number whereas cilia are shorter and less in number

320. **Choose the incorrect statement about the core of flagella:**

(a) It is made up of a number of microtubules running parallel to the long axis

(b) It consists of nine pairs of doublets of radially arranged peripheral microtubules

(c) It also has two pairs of centrally located microtubules

(d) The central microtubules are connected to each other by bridges

1. The term protoplasm was coined by:
   a. Robert Hooke
   b. Dujardin
   c. Robert Brown
   d. Purkinje

2. Which is correct about cell theory in view of the current status of our knowledge about cell structure?
   a. It needs modification due to the discovery of subcellular structures like chloroplasts and mitochondria
   b. Modified cell theory means that all living beings are composed of cells capable of reproducing
   c. Cell theory does not hold good because of exceptions like viruses as they do not have cellular organization
   d. Cell theory means that all living objects consist of cells whether or not capable of reproducing

3. Smaller cells have:
   a. Small surface area per volume ratio
   b. Large surface area per volume ratio
   c. Slow exchange rate of nutrients
   d. None of the above

4. Substance forming 80% of cytoplasm in plant cells is:
   a. Proteins
   b. Water
   c. Fats
   d. Minerals

5. Protoplasm forms a percentage of the total weight of the body:
   a. 45%
   b. 60%
   c. 95%
   d. 15%

6. Protoplasm is:
   a. Non-living matter
   b. Bearer of hereditary characters
   c. Living matter without function
   d. The physical basis of life

7. A protoplast is a cell: (AIPMT 2015)
   a. Without cell wall
   b. Without plasma membrane
   c. Without nucleus
   d. Undergoing division

8. Protoplast lacks: (Cht. 2015)
   a. Cytoplasm
   b. Nucleus
   c. Mitochondria
   d. Cell wall

9. Minimum cell size seen under light microscope is:
   a. 1 µm
   b. 0.1 µm
   c. 0.25 µm
   d. 0.5 µm

10. An exception to cell theory is:
   a. Mycoplasma
   b. Virus
   c. Protistans
   d. Algae

11. Physical basis of life is: (RPMT 2005)
   a. Nucleoplasm
   b. Cytoplasm
   c. Plasmalemma
   d. Protoplasm

12. Protoplasm is:
   a. Emulsion
   b. Complex colloidal solution
   c. Molecular solution
   d. Suspension

13. Which of the following components are separated by? (NEET 2017)
   a. Nuclear membrane
   b. Plasma membrane
   c. Glycocalyx
   d. Cell wall

14. Subcellular components are separated by: (Manipal 2009)
   a. Electrophoresis
   b. Cell fractionation
   c. Flow cytometry
   d. Autoradiography

15. Bacteria having tuft of flagella at both the poles are: (MPPMT 2012)
   a. Atrichous
   b. Peritrichous
   c. Lophotrichous
   d. Amphitrichous

16. Select the wrong statement: (NEET 2016)
   a. Cyanobacteria lack flagellated cells
   b. Mycoplasma is a well-less microorganism
   c. Bacterial cell wall is made up of peptidoglycan

d. Pili and fimbriae are mainly involved in the motility of bacterial cells

17. Choose the wrong statement regarding bacterial cells:

A. Glycocalyx is the outermost envelope in bacteria

B. Glycocalyx could be a loose sheath called capsule

C. Glycocalyx may be thick and tough called slime layer

D. A special structure formed by the plasma membrane is called mesosome

E. Small bristle-like fibers sprouting out the cell are called fimbriae:

a. A and C are wrong

b. A and B are wrong

c. B and C are wrong

d. A and D are wrong

18. Cork cells have a deposition of:

a. Pectin

b. Cutin

c. Suberin

d. Lignin

9. Pits found in the cell wall are due to lack of: (JKCMEE 2007)

a. Middle lamella

b. Cell plate

c. Primary wall material

d. Secondary wall material

0. Protoplasmic strands between adjacent plant cells are: (AFMC)

a. Ectodesmata

b. Desmosomes

c. Protoplasmic fibrils

d. Plasmodesmata

1. Which is correct in view of the fluid mosaic model?

(AIPMT 2008)

a. Proteins can flip-flop, lipids cannot

b. Neither protein nor lipids cannot flip-flop

c. Both lipids cannot and proteins can flip-flop

d. Lipids can rarely flip-flop, proteins cannot

22. Prokaryotic cell does not possess:

(Har PMT 2005)

a. Centrioles

b. Membrane bound organelles

c. Desmosomes

d. All the above

23. Adjacent cells are interconnected by: (AMU 2005)

a. Vacuoles

b. E. R

c. Desmosomes

d. Mitochondria

24. ATP is required for: (BHU 2007)

a. Active process

b. Passive process

c. All types of processes

d. None of the above

25. Which of the following does not differ in *E. coli* and *Chlamydomonas*? (AIPMT 2012)

a. Ribosomes

b. Chromosomal organization

c. Cell wall

d. Cell membrane

26. Fluidity of biomembrane is observed through: (DPMT 2009)

a. Tissue culture

b. Fluorescence microscope

c. Phase-contrast microscope

d. Electron microscope

27. Which is not a constituent of cell membrane?   (AIPMT 2007)

a. Glycolipids

b. Phospholipids

c. Cholesterol

d. Proline

28. Cell recognition and adhesion occur due to biochemicals of cell membranes named: (WB 2007)

a. Proteins

b. Lipids

c. Proteins and lipids

d. Glycoprotein and glycolipids

29. Bacteria with a tuft of flagella at one pole are:

a. Atrichous

b. Peritrichous

c. Lophotrichous

d. Amphitrichous

30. Most of the water found in the young cell occurs in:

a. Cell wall

b. Nucleus

c. Cytoplasm

d. Vacuoles

31. Pectin polysaccharide are present in:

a. Cytoskeleton

b. Plasma membrane

c. Primary cell wall

d. Secondary cell wall

32. Which is present to plasma membrane in plant cell?

a. Secondary wall

b. Primary wall

c. Middle lamella

d. Tonoplast

33. Desmosomes is a modification of:

a. E. R – nucleus complex

b. E. R

c. Golgi complex

d. Plasma membrane

34. Welded areas between two adjacent animal cells are:

a. Interdigitations

b. Desmosomes

c. Gap junctions

d. Intercellular bridges

35. According to fluid mosaic model plasma membrane is composed of:

a. Phospholipids and oligosaccharides

b. Phospholipids and hemicellulose

c. The phospholipid and integral protein

d. Phospholipid, extrinsic protein, and intrinsic protein

36. In Singer and Nicolson's model, the extrinsic proteins are:

a. Tightly associated with intrinsic proteins but can be easily separated

b. Loosely associated with intrinsic proteins and can be easily separated

c. Loosely associated with intrinsic proteins but cannot be easily separated

d. Tightly associated with intrinsic proteins and cannot be easily separated

37. Fluidity of cell membranes in cold weather is maintained by:
(PB PMT 2005)

a. Increase the number of phospholipids with unsaturated hydrocarbons tails

b. Increasing the proportion of integral proteins

c. Increasing concentration of cholesterol in membrane

d. Increasing the number of phospholipids with saturated hydrocarbon tails

38. Lipid molecules of the plasma membrane are arranged:

a. Alternately

b. In series

c. Parallel

d. Scattered

39. Assertion: A cell membrane shows fluid behavior.

Reason: A membrane is a mosaic of diverse lipids and proteins.
(AIIMS 2008)

a. Both Assertion and Reason are true and Reason is the correct explanation of Assertion.

b. Both Assertion and Reason are true but Reason is not the correct explanation of Assertion.

c. Assertion is true but Reason is false.

d. Assertion is false but Reason is true.

40. Which of the following is correct for transmembrane proteins in a lipid bilayer?   (WB JEE 2015)

a. They are absent in plant animal cells.

b. They act as channel proteins

c. They are absent in plant cells

d. They are only externally located

41. Which is not a part of endomembrane system?
(AIPMT 2011)

a. Golgi body

b. Vacuole

c. Peroxisome

d. Lysosome

42. E. R of rapidly diving cells is:

a. Non-functional

b. Poorly developed

c. Absent

d. Highly developed

43. E. R is more developed in:

a. Green cells

b. Young cells

c. Mature cells

d. Bacteriophage cells

44. The main organelles involved in the modification and routing of newly synthesized proteins to their destination is:
(JIPMER 2007)

a. Mitochondria

b. E. R

c. Chloroplast

d. Lysosome

45. Golgi apparatus absent in:

a. Higher plants

b. Yeast

c. Bacteria and cyano-bacteria

d. Liver cells

46. The Golgi complex plays a major role: (NEET 2013)

a. In trapping the light and transforming it into chemical energy

b. In digesting proteins and carbohydrates

c. As energy transferring organelles

d. In the post-translation modification of proteins and glycosylation of lipids

47. Golgi apparatus commonly present in:

a. Near mitochondria

b. Near chloroplast

c. Perinuclear area

d. Germ cells

48. Main function of dictyosome is:
(CPMT 2005)

a. Storage

b. Respiration

c. Secretion

d. Breakdown of fat

49. Dictyosome is absent in:
(AIIMS 2012)

a. Cyanobacteria

b. Mycoplasma

c. Bacteria

d. All of the above

50. Golgi complex is specialized for:

a. Glycosylation of lipids and proteins

b. Conservation of light energy into chemical energy

c. Energy transduction

d. Digestion of carbohydrates and protein

51. Cells with secretory function have abundant:

a. Dictyosome

b. E. R

c. Lysosomes

d. Mitochondria

52. Functions of Golgi apparatus are:

(A) Transport and modified materials.

(B) Secretes mucin in respiratory tract

(C) Secretes slime in insectivorous plants

What is correct?

a. Wrong – (A), Correct - (B) and (C)

b. Wrong – (B), Correct - (A) and (C)

c. Wrong – (B) and (C), Correct - (A)

d. Wrong – nil, Correct - All

53. Which cell organelles reduce the number of other organelles?

a. Oxysomes

b. Lysosomes

c. Mitochondria

d. None of these

54. When a lysosome fuses with a phagosome, it results in the formation of:

a. Secondary lysosome

b. Primary lysosome

c. Autophagic vacuole

d. Residual body

55. Which of the following in lysosome? **(DPMT 2007)**

a. Basic phosphatase

b. Acid phosphatase

c. Oxidoreductase

d. Lyase

56. Heterophagosome is:

(Odisha 2012)

a. Lysosome in which only indigestible food is left

b. Formed by the fusion of primary lysosome with degenerating intracellular organelles

c. Newly pinched out vesicle from Golgi apparatus which fused with endosome to become functional

d. Formed by the fusion of primary lysosome with food containing phagosome

57. Which is incorrect in relation to lysosomes?

a. They contain acid hydrolases

b. They are autophagic

c. They can digest proteins, nucleic acid, lipids, and polysaccharides

d. They are monomorphic

58. Water-soluble pigment present in cell vacuole is:

a. Anthocyanin

b. Carotene

c. Xanthophyll

d. Chlorophyll

59. Colours of flower petals is due to:

(Chd. CET 2011)

a. Xanthophyll

b. Carotenes

c. Anthocyanin

d. Phycoerythrin

60. These types of vacuoles contain hydrolases:

a. Sap

b. Contractile

c. Food

d. Air

61. Mitochondria do not occur in:

(AFMC 2009)

a. Human liver cell

b. Human nerve cell

c. Human erythrocyte cell

d. Frog liver cell

62. Outer and inner membrane of mitochondria are:

a. Structurally and functionally similar

b. Structurally and functionally dissimilar

c. Structurally similar but functionally dissimilar

d. Structurally dissimilar but functionally similar

63. Mitochondria are absent in:

a. Bacteria

b. Red algae

c. Green algae

d. Brown algae

64. ETC is a component of:

a. Golgi apparatus

b. Mitochondria

c. Nucleus

d. Microtubule

65. Read the two statements, (A) and (B):

Statement (A): The number of mitochondria in a cell does not correspond to the function of the cell.

Statement (B): Mitochondria are common to both plant and animal cells.

Choose the correct option from following: **(KCET 2006)**

a. Both the statements are correct

b. Both the statements are wrong

c. Statement (A) is correct but (B) is wrong

d. Statement (B) is correct but (A) is wrong

66. Which of the following statement regarding to mitochondrial membrane is not correct?
(AIPMT 2006)

a. Outer membrane resembles to sieve

b. Outer membrane is permeable to all kinds of molecules

c. Enzymes of electron transport chain are embedded in outer membrane

d. Inner membrane is highly convoluted forming a series of infoldings

67. Mitochondria and chloroplasts are considered to be endosymbionts of cells because they:

a. Do not arise *de novo*

b. Possess their own nucleic acid s

c. Have membranes similar to those of bacteria

d. All of the above

68. Which statement is not correct with reference to mitochondria?
(KCET 2009)

a. They divide in synchrony with cell cycle

b. They contain DNA

c. They contain cristae

d. They provide chemical energy

69. Mitochondria will be found in abundance in cells of tissues having: **(Manipal 2013)**

a. Minimum activity

b. Average activity

c. Maximum activity

d. None of these

70. Oxysomes or $F_0 - F_1$ particles occur on:

a. Thylakoids

b. Mitochondrial surface

c. Inner mitochondrial membrane

d. Chloroplast surface

71. Mitochondria performs all functions except: **(Cht. 2015)**

a. Nucleic acid synthesis

b. Steroid synthesis

c. ATP synthesis

d. Polysaccharide degradation

72. Inner membrane of mitochondria possesses:

a. $F_0 - F_1$ particles

b. ATPase

c. TCA enzyme

d. All of the above

73. What is mitoplast? **(WB 2010)**

a. Membrane less mitochondria

b. Mitochondria without inner membrane

c. Another name of mitochondria

d. Mitochondria without outer membrane

74. Small particles projecting from inner surface of cristae and inner mitochondrial membrane are:
(WB 2008)

a. Microsomes

b. Oxysomes

c. Myeloid bodies

d. Informosomes

75. Which is wrong? **(AIPMT 2007)**

a. Both chloroplast and mitochondrion have an internal compartment or thylakoid space bound by thylakoid membrane

b. Both contain DNA

c. Chloroplast is generally larger

d. Both are covered by a double membrane

76. Mitochondria and chloroplast are:
(NEET 2016)

(A) Semi-autonomous organelles

(B) Formed by division of pre-existing organelles and they contain DNA but lack protein synthesizing machinery.

Which one of the following options is correct?

a. Both (A) and (B) are correct

b. (B) is true, (A) is false

c. (A) is true, (B) is false

d. Both (A) and (B) are false

77. The term thylakoid was coined by:

a. Arnon

b. Park and Biggins

c. Menke

d. Willstatter

78. Which is common between chloroplast, chromoplast and leucoplasts? **(AIIMS 2006)**

a. Presence of pigments

b. Presence of thylakoids and grana

c. Storage of starch, proteins and lipids

d. Ability to multiply by a fission like process

79. Which is mismatched?
(Kerala 2007)

a. Amyloplast – Store protein granules

b. Elaioplast – Store oil or fat

c. Chloroplast – Contain chlorophyll pigments

d. Chromoplast – Contains pigments other than chlorophyll

80. Agranal chloroplasts are found in some:

a. Succulents

b. Hydrophytes

c. C$_3$ plants

d. C$_4$ plants

81. Lipid content of chloroplast is:

(MPPMT 2011)

a. 20 – 30%

b. 5 – 10%

c. 4 – 5%

d. 1 – 2%

82. Assertion: Mitochondria and chloroplasts are semiautonomous organelles.
Reason: They are formed by division of pre-existing organelles as well as contain DNA but lack protein synthesizing machinery.

(AIIMS 2005)

a. Both Assertion and Reason are true and Reason is the correct explanation of Assertion.

b. Both Assertion and Reason are true but Reason is not correct explanation of Assertion.

c. Assertion is true but Reason is false.

d. Assertion is false but Reason is true.

83. The subunits pf ribosome remains united at a critical ion level of:

(AIPMT 2008)

a. Copper

b. Manganese

c. Magnesium

d. Calcium

84. Ribosomes is often called:

(NEET 2016)

a. Microsome

b. RNA particle

c. Dictyosome

d. Oxysomes

85. Microtubules are constituents of:

(NEET 2016)

a. Cilia, Flagella and Peroxisome

b. Spindle fibers, Centrioles and Cilia

c. Centrioles, Spindle fibers and Chromatin

d. Centrosomes, Nucleosome and Centrioles

86. Conversion of green tomatoes into red form involves:

a. Formation of chromoplasts from chloroplasts

b. Destruction of chloroplasts and development of chromoplasts from leucoplasts

c. Formation of chromoplasts from leucoplasts

d. All of the above

87. Nucleus is absent in:

a. Companion cells

b. Sieve tube cells

c. Phloem parenchyma

d. Cambium

88. Chromatin is chemically made of:

(WB 2009)

a. Nucleic acid, histone and non-histone proteins

b. Nucleic acid and histone proteins

c. Nucleic acid and non-histone proteins

d. Nucleic acid

89. Assertion: The true nucleus is generally absent in *E. coli* and other prokaryotes.
Reason: An undifferentiated, unorganized fibrillar nucleus without any limiting membrane is observed in prokaryotic cells.

(AIIMS 2007)

a. Both Assertion and Reason are true and Reason is the correct explanation of Assertion.

b. Both Assertion and Reason are true but Reason is not correct explanation of Assertion.

c. Assertion is true but Reason is false.

d. Assertion is false but Reason is true.

90. Extracellular chromosome occurs in:

(CPMT 2012)

a. Peroxisome and ribosomes

b. Chloroplast and mitochondria

c. Mitochondria and ribosome

d. Chloroplast and lysosome

91. The term chromosome was coined by:

a. Hofmeister

b. Strasburger

c. Waldeyer

d. Leeuwenhoek

92. Karyotype is: **(CPMT 2009)**

a. Division of nucleus

b. Chromosome complement specific for each species

c. All organisms possessing some type of chromosomes

d. None of the above

93. Proteins required for functioning of nucleus are formed in:

(BHU 2012)

a. Cytoplasm

b. R.E.R

c. Nucleolus

d. Mitochondria

94. Nuclear envelope is a derivative of: **(AIPMT 2015)**

a. R.E.R

b. S.E.R

c. Membrane of Golgi complex

d. Microtubules

95. Extrachromosomal DNA occurs in:

(AFMC 2012)

a. Mitochondria

b. Ribosomes

c. Nucleus

d. Chromosomes

96. The term lipochondria was suggested for: (MPPMT 2011)

a. Mitochondria

b. Golgi complex

c. E.R

d. All of these

97. Select the correct statements:

(A) Endomembrane system includes plasma membrane, ER, Golgi complex, lysosomes and vacuoles.

(B) ER helps in transport of substances, synthesis of proteins, lipoproteins and glycogen

(C) Ribosomes are involved in protein synthesis

(D) Mitochondria help in oxidative phosphorylation and generation of ATP

(Kerala 2011)

a. (B), (C) and (D) are correct

b. Alone (A) correct

c. Alone (B) correct

d. Alone (C) correct

98. Select the mismatch:

(NEET 2016)

a. Gas vacuole – Green bacterial cells

b. Large central vacuoles – Animal cells

c. Protists – Eukaryotes

d. Methanogens – Prokaryotes

99. TCA enzyme mostly occurs in:

(Odisha 2011)

a. Ribosomes

b. Mitochondrial matrix

c. Cytoplasm

d. Peroxisome

100. The technique that separates proteins according to their molecular weight:

a. PAGE

b. Affinity chromatography

c. Ion exchange chromatography

d. Gel filtration

101. Organelle involved in transformation of cell membrane is:

a. E. R

b. Lysosome

c. Golgisome

d. Mesosome

102. Organelle connected with glycosylation of proteins is:

(AIIMS)

a. Ribosome

b. E. R

c. Mitochondria

d. Chloroplast

103. Balbiani rings are sites of:

a. RNA and protein synthesis

b. Lipid synthesis

c. Nucleotide synthesis

d. Polysaccharide synthesis

104. What is not true of Sphaerosomes?

a. Single membrane covering

b. Connected with fats

c. Arise from E. R

d. Involved in photorespiration

105. Plant cells store fat in:

(Kerala 2005)

a. Peroxisome

b. Lysosome

c. Sphaerosomes

d. Microsome

106. Sphaerosomes have:

(Odisha 2008)

a. Cellulose reserve

b. Protein reserve

c. Lipid reserve

d. Both protein and lipid reserve

107. Which of the following is covered by a single membrane?

a. Nucleus

b. Mitochondria

c. Plastids

d. Sphaerosomes

108. Peroxisome occur in:

a. Bundle sheath

b. Vascular bundle

c. Mesophyll cells

d. Endosperm

109. Polymorphic cell organelle is:

a. Glyoxysomes

b. Peroxisome

c. Lysosome

d. Golgi complex

110. Which is distributed more widely in a cell?

a. DNA

b. RNA

c. Chloroplast

d. Sphaerosomes

111. Assertion: it is important that organisms have cells.

Reason: A cell keeps its chemical composition steady within its boundary.   (AIIMS)

a. Both Assertion and Reason are true and Reason is the correct explanation of Assertion.

b. Both Assertion and Reason are true but Reason is not correct explanation of Assertion.

c. Assertion is true but Reason is false.

d. Assertion is false but Reason is true.

112. Select the mismatch:

(NEET 2016)

a. Protists – Eukaryotes

b. Methanogens – Prokaryotes

c. Gas vacuoles – Green bacteria

d. Large central vacuoles – Animal cells

113. Cell organelle taking part in photorespiration is:

a. Glyoxysomes

b. Peroxisome

c. Dictyosome

d. E. R

114. Glyoxysomes are concerned with metabolism of:

a. Fats

b. Proteins

c. Carbohydrates

d. All of these

115. The function of peroxisome is:

(Chhattisgarh 2015)

a. To convert H_2O_2 into H_2O and O_2

b. Utilization of O_2 gas

c. To break toxic molecules of a cell

d. All of these

116. Recent researches suggest that peroxisomes have .... origin.

a. Cyanobacterial

b. Fusobacterial

c. Proteobacterial

d. Actinobacterial

117. GERL system is found of:

(Chhattisgarh 2015)

a. Golgi body, endoplasmic reticulum, ribosome, and lysosome

b. Golgi body, endoplasmic reticulum, and lysosome

c. Golgi body, endoplasmic reticulum, and ribosome

d. Golgi body, lysosome and ribosome

118. GERL is associated with:

a. Cell membrane

b. Golgi body

c. Mitochondrion

d. Chloroplast

119. Which one is correctly matched?

a. F1 particles – ribosome

b. Lysosome – acrosome

c. Ribosome – single membrane

d. Chlorophyll A and chlorophyll B – chloroplast

120. An oxidative organelle is:

(CET Chd 2011)

a. Ribosome

b. Golgi body

c. Peroxisome

d. E.R

121. Circular DNA occurs in:

a. Bacteria only

b. Bacteria and chloroplast

c. All viruses

d. Bacteria, chloroplasts, and mitochondria

122. The osmotic expansion of a cell kept in water is chiefly regulated by: **(AIPMT 2014)**

a. Plastids

b. Ribosomes

c. Mitochondria

d. Vacuoles

123. Colour of Rose petals is due to water soluble pigment present in:

a. Cytoplasm

b. Intercellular space

c. Nucleus

d. Vacuoles

124. Cuticle occurs over:

(Odisha 2007)

a. Virus

b. Human cell

c. Plant cell

d. Bacterium

125. Membrane most abundant in a cell is: **(WB 2008)**

a. Nuclear membrane

b. Golgi membrane

c. Plasma membrane

d. E. R membrane

126. In cytosis the cell: **(KCET 2009)**

a. Divides cytoplasm in mitosis

b. Digests itself

c. Engulfs and internalizes materials with its membrane

d. Enables extracellular digestion of larger molecules

127. In which of the following would you expect to find Glyoxysomes? **(AIIMS 2005)**

a. Endosperm of Wheat

b. Endosperm of castor

c. Palisade cell in leaf

d. Root hair

128. In an animal cell, protein synthesis takes place: **(AFMC 2007)**

a. Only on the ribosomes present in the cytosol

b. Only on the ribosomes attached to the nuclear envelope and endoplasmic reticulum

c. On ribosomes present in the nucleolus as well as the cytoplasm

d. On ribosomes present in the cytosol as well as the mitochondria

129. Match the column I to column II and identify the correct option: **(AIPMT 2015)**

Column – I	Column – II
(A) Thylakoid	(i) Disc-shaped sacs Golgi apparatus
(B) Cristae	(ii) Condensed structure of DNA
(C) Cisternae	(iii) Flat membranous sacs in stroma

(D) Chromatin	(iv) Infoldings in mitochondria

a. (A) – (iii), (B) – (iv), (C) – (ii), (D) – (i)

b. (A) – (iv), (B) – (iii), (C) – (i), (D) – (ii)

c. (A) – (iii), (B) – (iv), (C) – (i), (D) – (ii)

d. (A) – (iii), (B) – (i), (C) – (iv), (D) – (ii)

130. A membranous bag with hydrolytic enzymes used for controlling intracellular digestion of macromolecules is:

a. Endoplasmic reticulum

b. Nucleosome

c. Lysosome

d. Phagosome

131. The common feature amongst nucleus, chloroplast, and mitochondria is:

a. Lamellae

b. DNA

c. Cristae

d. All of these

132. Which is the correct option amongst the following statements?

(A) Nuclear membrane, chloroplast, mitochondria, microtubules, and pili are absent in prokaryotic cells.

(B) Nuclear membrane, chloroplast, mitochondria, microtubules, and pili are present in eukaryotic cells.

(C) Ribosomes are 70S in prokaryotic cells and mitochondria, as they are 80S in animal cells.

a. (A) and (B) are wrong, (C) is correct

b. (B) and (C) are wrong, (A) is correct

c. (B) is wrong, (A) and (C) are correct

d. (A), (B) and (C) are wrong

133. Which one is wrong statement regarding cell organelles?

(AIIMS 2005)

a. Lysosomes are double membrane vesicles budded off from Golgi bodies and contain digestive enzymes

b. E. R consist of a network of membranous tubules helps in transport, synthesis and secretion

c. Leucoplasts have their own DNA and protein synthesizing machinery

d. Sphaerosomes are single membrane bound and are associated with synthesis and storage of lipids

134. Which of these organelles does not contain ribosomes?

I.   **Rough endoplasmic reticulum**

II. **Chloroplast**

III. **Golgi Apparatus**

IV. **Mitochondria**

Select the correct answer using codes given below:

a. I and IV

b. I and III

c. Only IV

d. II, III and IV

135. A cell organelle with folded inner membrane is disrupted with ultrasonic breaker. Its fragments can synthesize ATP. The organelle is:

a. Ribosome

b. Centrosome

c. Chloroplast

d. Mitochondrion

136. Pick up the correct answer:

(BHU 2008)

1. **Mitochondrion contains DNA**

2. **70S ribosomes occur in prokaryotes**

3. **Ribosomes are made up of phospholipids and oligosaccharides**

4. **Ribosomes are not found in Protista and Monera**

a. 1, 2, and 3 are correct

b. 1, 2 are correct

c. 2, 4 are correct

d. 1, 3 are correct

137. Which one does not contain DNA?   **(MPPMT 2009)**

a. Peroxisome

b. Nucleus

c. Chloroplast

d. Mitochondria

138. The long and short arm of chromosomes are designated respectively as: **(DPMT 2010)**

a. p and q

b. q and p

c. α and β

d. m and p

139. Assertion: Specialization of cells is advantageous to organisms. Reason: It increase the operational efficiency.

a. Both Assertion and Reason are true and Reason is the correct explanation of Assertion.

b. Both Assertion and Reason are true but Reason is not correct explanation of Assertion.

c. Assertion is true but Reason is false.

d. Assertion is false but Reason is true.

140. Pectin occurs in:

(Manipal 2005)

a. Blood proteins

b. Plant cell wall

c. Milk protein

d. Liver cell

141. Cell organelle covered by single unit membrane is:

a. Glyoxysome

b. Lysosome

c. Peroxisome

d. All of these

142. Cellular totipotency means:

a. Synthesis of new cell

b. Formation of new species

c. Formation of new plants

d. Capacity of plants cell to form complete plant

143. Cellular totipotency is demonstrated by:

a. Only gymnosperm plants

b. All plant cells

c. All animal cells

d. Only bacterial cells

144. Matched the following and choose the correct answer:

(AIPMT 2014)

(A) Centriole – (i) Infoldings in mitochondria

(B) Chlorophyll – (ii) Thylakoids

(C) Cristae – (iii) Nucleic acid

(D) Ribozymes – (iv) Basal body of cilia and flagella

a. (A) – (i), (B) – (iii), (C) – (ii), (D) – (iv)

b. (A) – (iv), (B) – (iii), (C) – (i), (D) – (ii)

c. (A) – (iv), (B) – (ii), (C) – (i), (D) – (iii)

d. (A) – (i), (B) – (ii), (C) – (iv), (D) – (iii)

145. Messenger RNA (mRNA) is formed in: **(CPMT 2005)**

a. Nucleus

b. E. R

c. Ribosomes

d. Golgi apparatus

146. Which one is an organelle with in an organelle? **(AIPMT 2012)**

a. E. R

b. Ribosome

c. Peroxisome

a. Mesosome

147. March the column I to Column II and choose the correct option:

(Kerala 2008)

Column I	Column II
(A) E. R	(i) Stack of cisternae
(B) Sphaerosomes	(ii) Store oil
(C) Dictyosome	(iii) Synthesis and storage of lipids
(D) Peroxisomes	(iv) Photorespiration
(E) Elaioplast	(v) Detoxification of blood

a. (A) – (v), (B) – (iii), (C) – (i), (D) – (iv), (E) – (ii)

b. (A) – (v), (B) – (iii), (C) – (ii), (D) – (iv), (E) – (i)

c. (A) – (ii), (B) – (iii), (C) – (i), (D) – (iv), (E) – (v)

d. (A) – (iii), (B) – (iv), (C) – (i), (D) – (v), (E) – (ii)

EXERCISE 3

Difficulty Level: Hard

1. Schleiden (1838) proposed a cell to be the structural and functional unit of life. His idea is

a. Observation

b. Assumption

c. Generalization

d. Hypothesis

2. When a cell of 2μm diameter grows to double its diameter, its surface area, volume relationship will: **(KCET 2005)**

a. Remain the same

b. Become double

c. Reduce to half

d. Become undetermined

3. Streaming of cytoplasm within a living cell is: **(CET Chd 2011)**

a. Homoeostasis

b. Cyclosis

c. Diffusion

d. Osmoregulation

4. Which one shows streaming movements of protoplasm with in living cells? **(Har PMT 2007)**

a. Sensitive plant

b. Pith cells

c. Onion peeling

d. Staminal hair of *Tradescantia*

5. Gel part below the plasma membrane is:

a. Ectoplasm

b. Endoplasm

c. Plasmalemma

d. None of these

6. **Assertion: Eukaryotic cells have the ability to adopt a variety of shapes and carry out directed movements.**

   Reason: There are three principal types protein filaments, microfilaments, microtubules, and intermediate filaments and intermediate filaments which constitute the cytoskeleton.

   (AIIMS 2006)

   a. Both Assertion and Reason are true and Reason is the correct explanation of Assertion.

   b. Both Assertion and Reason are true but Reason is not correct explanation of Assertion.

   c. Assertion is true but Reason is false.

   d. Assertion is false but Reason is true.

7. **Which of the following statements are false?**

   (Kerala 2006)

   (A) Most cells are tiny with volume range of 1-100 nm^3

   (B) Some cells have microvilli to increase the absorptive surface area

   (C) All cells arise from pre-existing cells

   (D) In plants, translocation of solutes in performed by xylem vessels and tracheids

   (E) According to cell theory, all cells arise from abiotic material

   a. (A), (C) and (E) are false

   b. (A), (D) and (E) are false

   c. (B), (C) and (D) are false

   d. (C), (D) and (E) are false

8. **Smallest unit of plant cell wall is:**

   (AMU 2015)

   a. Micelle

   b. Microfibril

   c. Fibril

   d. None of these

9. **N-acetyl muramic acid is found in:**

   (WB 2012)

   a. Cell wall of plants

   b. Cell wall of bacteria

   c. Cell wall of fungi

   d. Viral coat

10. **Functions of Na$^+$ -K$^+$ pump enable:**

    (Odisha 2009)

    a. Na$^+$ out and Cl$^-$ in

    b. Cl$^-$ out and Na$^+$ in

    c. Na$^+$ in and K$^+$ out

    d. Na$^+$ out and K$^+$ in

11. **Detoxification of lipid soluble drugs and other harmful compounds in ER is carried out by cytochrome:**

    (AMU 2011)

    a. $a_1 - a_3$

    b. c

    c. b_f

    d. P_{450}

12. **Detoxification site in liver is:**

    a. Free ribosome

    b. Golgi complex

    c. SER

    d. RER

13. **Nissl granules are formed from:**

    a. RER

    b. SER

    c. DNA

    d. Golgi body

14. **Which organelle is only present in plants?**

a. Glyoxysome

b. Lysosome

c. Peroxisome

d. Ribosome

15. **Which one is does not occur in cell vacuole?**

    a. Hydrolytic enzyme

    b. Latex

    c. Anthocyanins

    d. DNA

16. **Glycolate metabolism occurs in:**

    a. Lysosome

    b. Ribosome

    c. Glyoxysome

    d. Peroxisome

17. **Apparato reticulo interno was discovered by C. Golgi in:**

    a. 1898

    b. 1900

    c. 1925

    d. 1928

18. **A clear zone around Golgi apparatus is:**

    (JKCMEE 2011)

    a. Zone of separation

    b. Zone of transition

    c. Zone of inclusion

    d. Zone of exclusion

19. **Phagocytosis first seen by:**

    a. Huxley

    b. Strasburger

    c. Haeckel

    d. Metchnikoff

20. **Quantasomes occur in:**

    a. Stroma

    b. Grana/Chloroplast

    c. Golgi body

    d. Mitochondria

21. **Chloroplast of algae lack:**

    a. Quantasomes

    b. Lamellae

    c. Pigments

d. Grana

22. **Ribosomes are essential for protein synthesis, but they are present in mitochondria and plastids, the sites of respiration and photosynthesis. What is the role of ribosomes in these organelles?**

(EAMCET 2015)

a. Ribosomes transport ATP formed in respiration and photosynthesis to cytoplasm through ER
b. Subunits of some required proteins are synthesized in these organelles
c. Ribosome transport RNA and DNA to cytoplasm
d. All of these

23. **Experiments to demonstrate importance of nucleus in controlling growth and heredity were performed on:**

a. *Acetabularia*
b. *Neurospora*
c. Leucocytes
d. Starfish egg

24. **Which of the following subunits of ribosomes is composed of 23S rRNA and a 5S rRNA plus thirty-four different proteins?**

a. 30S
b. 40S
c. 50S
d. 60S

25. **House-keeping proteins occur in:**

(AMU 2010)

a. Golgi complex
b. Cytoskeleton
c. E.R
d. All of these

26. **Telomere repetitive DNA sequence control the function of eukaryotic chromosome because they:** **(AFMC 2012)**

a. Act as replicants
b. rRNA transcription factors
c. Help in chromosome pairing
d. Prevent chromosome loss

27. **Lampbrush chromosomes occur inside:** **(BHU 2008)**

a. Nucleus of human cells
b. Oocytes of amphibians
c. Salivary glands of *Drosophila*
d. Salivary gland of silk moth

28. **Points at which polytene chromosomes appear attached is:**

a. Centriole
b. Chromocenter
c. Centromere
d. Centrosome

29. **Polytene chromosome were discovered in:** **(BHU 2012)**

a. *Chironomus*
b. *Drosophila*
c. Musca
d. Culex

30. **Which one possesses giant chromosomes?** **(WB JEE 2012)**

a. *Drosophila*
b. *Xenopsylla*
c. *Branchiomyces*
d. Mouse

31. **In ideogram, chromosomes of an organism are arranged according to their:**

a. Increasing size
b. Decreasing size
c. Position of centromere
d. Number of centromeres

32. **In germinating seeds, fatty acids are arranged exclusively in the:**

(AIPMT 2008)

a. Proplastids
b. Glyoxysomes
c. Peroxisomes
d. Mitochondria

33. **Gluconeogenesis occurs in:**

(Odisha 2008)

a. Golgi bodies
b. Glyoxysomes
c. Mitochondria
d. Lysosomes

34. **Pick up the correct answer about idioblast:** **(BHU 2008)**

1. Plant cell different from others
2. Animal cell different from others
3. Plant cell having cell inclusions
4. Animal cell having cell inclusions

a. 1, 2 and 3 are correct
b. 1 and 2 are correct
c. 2 and 4 are correct
d. 1 and 3 are correct

35. **A thoroughly washed beet root slice kept in water at room temperature does not lose anthocyanin pigment because plasma membrane is:**

a. Permeable to anthocyanin
b. Impermeable to anthocyanin
c. Selectively permeable to anthocyanin
d. Dead

36. **Disappearance of tadpole tail during metamorphosis is brought about by:** **(AMU 2010)**

a. Lysosome
b. Peroxisomes
c. Golgi apparatus
d. Endoplasmic reticulum

37. **Match the following:**

(Kerala 2006)

(A) Bacteria	(i) Synthesis and storage of lipids	
(B) Sphaerosomes	(ii) Idiogram	
(C) Chloroplast	(iii) Glycocalyx	
(D) Karyotype	(iv) Thylakoids	

a. (A) – (iii), (B) – (i), (C) – (iv), (D) – (ii)
b. (A) – (iii), (B) – (i), (C) – (ii), (D) – (iv)
c. (A) – (iv), (B) – (iii), (C) – (ii), (D) – (i)
d. (A) – (i), (B) – (ii), (C) – (iii), (D) – (iv)

38. Centre for phosphorylation is:
a. Ribosome
b. Oxysomes
c. Peroxisome
d. Sphaerosomes

39. The organelles present in germinating seeds and connected with β-oxidation or fat digestion is:
a. Glyoxysome
b. Sphaerosomes
c. Peroxisome
d. Mitochondrion

40. Match the columns:

(Kerala 2006)

Column I	Column II
(A) Sap vacuole	1. Contain digestive enzymes
(B) Contractile vacuole	2. Store metabolic gases
(C) Food vacuole	3. Osmoregulation
(D) Air vacuole	4. Store lipids
(E) Sphaerosomes	5. Store and concentrates minerals salts and nutrients

a. (A) – 5, (B) – 3, (C) – 1, (D) – 2, (E) – 4
b. (A) – 2, (B) – 3, (C) – 4, (D) – 5, (E) - 1
c. (A) – 5, (B) – 2, (C) – 3, (D) – 1, (E) - 4
d. (A) – 5, (B) – 3, (C) – 2, (D) – 4, (E) – 1

41. Fernandez-Moran particles are found in: **(Odisha 2012)**
a. Golgi bodies
b. Chromosomes
c. Mitochondria
d. Nucleus

42. Which of the following plant cells is not surrounded by cell wall?

(MPPMT 2009)
a. Root hair cell
b. Stem hair cell
c. Gamete cell
d. Bacterial cell

43. Scanning electron microscope was invented by:
a. Lehmann
b. Max Hettinger
c. Marvin Minsky
d. Knoll and Ruska

44. Phase contrast micrograph was invented by: **(KCET 2009)**
a. Fritz-Zernike
b. Galileo Galilei
c. M. Knoll and E. Ruska
d. H Hansen and Z Jansen

45. What kind of microscopy uses acridine orange?   **(BCECE 2015)**
a. Phase contrast
b. Fluorescence
c. Transmission microscope
d. Scanning electron microscope

46. Which one is stained using carmine?   **(MPPMT 2012)**
a. Bacteria
b. Chromosomes
c. Diatoms
d. Viruses

47. Name the technique other than microscopy used for the study of the cell: **(PB PMT 2009)**
a. Obliteration
b. Plasmolysis
c. Flow cytometry
d. None of these

48. Protein substances are generally stained with:
a. Iodine
b. Light green
c. Cotton blue
d. Ruthenium red

49. At what speed, the mitochondria can be separated out by differential centrifugation?
a. 200 x g
b. 800 x g
c. 500 x g
d. 8000 x g

50. The following is generally used for creating density gradient centrifugation: **(BCECE 2015)**
a. NaCl
b. KCl
c. CsCl
d. $MgCl_2$

EXERCISE 1

1. (a)	41. (a)	81. (d)	121. (b)	161. (c)	201. (a)	241. (a)	281. (d)
2. (b)	42. (d)	82. (c)	122. (d)	162. (b)	202. (c)	242. (b)	282. (a)
3. (a)	43. (a)	83. (c)	123. (d)	163. (b)	203. (d)	243. (b)	283. (a)
4. (a)	44. (c)	84. (d)	124. (c)	164. (c)	204. (d)	244. (d)	284. (d)
5. (b)	45. (b)	85. (b)	125. (a)	165. (b)	205. (a)	245. (b)	285. (d)
6. (b)	46. (a)	86. (c)	126. (d)	166. (c)	206. (d)	246. (c)	286. (d)
7. (c)	47. (c)	87. (a)	127. (c)	167. (c)	207. (b)	247. (d)	287. (a)
8. (c)	48. (c)	88. (b)	128. (a)	168. (a)	208. (c)	248. (a)	288. (c)
9. (b)	49. (d)	89. (d)	129. (c)	169. (d)	209. (a)	249. (d)	289. (d)
10. (b)	50. (c)	90. (d)	130. (a)	170. (b)	210. (c)	250. (a)	290. (a)
11. (b)	51. (c)	91. (a)	131. (a)	171. (d)	211. (d)	251. (c)	291. (d)
12. (a)	52. (a)	92. (b)	132. (b)	172. (d)	212. (d)	252. (b)	292. (b)
13. (a)	53. (a)	93. (a)	133. (a)	173. (a)	213. (a)	253. (a)	293. (b)
14. (a)	54. (c)	94. (d)	134. (d)	174. (c)	214. (a)	254. (a)	294. (c)
15. (c)	55. (d)	95. (b)	135. (a)	175. (c)	215. (c)	255. (a)	295. (a)
16. (c)	56. (c)	96. (a)	136. (d)	176. (b)	216. (c)	256. (a)	296. (d)
17. (c)	57. (a)	97. (d)	137. (c)	177. (a)	217. (a)	257. (c)	297. (b)
18. (c)	58. (a)	98. (d)	138. (c)	178. (c)	218. (c)	258. (b)	298. (a)
19. (c)	59. (a)	99. (d)	139. (a)	179. (c)	219. (d)	259. (b)	299. (c)
20. (c)	60. (c)	100. (c)	140. (a)	180. (b)	220. (d)	260. (d)	300. (c)
21. (a)	61. (b)	101. (a)	141. (b)	181. (d)	221. (d)	261. (d)	301. (a)
22. (c)	62. (c)	102. (b)	142. (a)	182. (c)	222. (b)	262. (d)	302. (a)
23. (d)	63. (c)	103. (a)	143. (b)	183. (b)	223. (a)	263. (b)	303. (c)
24. (b)	64. (d)	104. (c)	144. (c)	184. (b)	224. (d)	264. (c)	304. (b)
25. (b)	65. (a)	105. (d)	145. (a)	185. (c)	225. (a)	265. (a)	305. (b)
26. (b)	66. (b)	106. (d)	146. (c)	186. (a)	226. (b)	266. (a)	306. (a)
27. (d)	67. (c)	107. (d)	147. (c)	187. (d)	227. (a)	267. (d)	307. (a)
28. (c)	68. (a)	108. (b)	148. (d)	188. (a)	228. (a)	268. (b)	308. (c)
29. (b)	69. (c)	109. (d)	149. (c)	189. (a)	229. (a)	269. (a)	309. (a)
30. (b)	70. (c)	110. (b)	150. (d)	190. (a)	230. (b)	270. (b)	310. (c)
31. (a)	71. (d)	111. (d)	151. (b)	191. (c)	231. (b)	271. (c)	311. (a)
32. (d)	72. (d)	112. (a)	152. (d)	192. (d)	232. (c)	272. (d)	312. (b)
33. (d)	73. (a)	113. (b)	153. (b)	193. (b)	233. (c)	273. (c)	313. (c)
34. (a)	74. (c)	114. (d)	154. (a)	194. (d)	234. (d)	274. (c)	314. (a)
35. (c)	75. (a)	115. (c)	155. (b)	195. (d)	235. (b)	275. (d)	315. (c)
36. (b)	76. (b)	116. (a)	156. (b)	196. (c)	236. (c)	276. (a)	316. (d)
37. (a)	77. (b)	117. (c)	157. (d)	197. (c)	237. (c)	277. (c)	317. (c)
38. (a)	78. (c)	118. (d)	158. (b)	198. (a)	238. (a)	278. (b)	318. (b)
39. (b)	79. (a)	119. (b)	159. (c)	199. (c)	239. (b)	279. (d)	319. (d)
40. (d)	80. (b)	120. (b)	160. (c)	200. (a)	240. (c)	280. (c)	320. (c)

1.	(d)	28.	(d)	55.	(d)	82.	(a)	109.	(b)	136.	(d)
2.	(c)	29.	(c)	56.	(b)	83.	(c)	110.	(c)	137.	(b)
3.	(b)	30.	(c)	57.	(a)	84.	(c)	111.	(b)	138.	(a)
4.	(b)	31.	(c)	58.	(b)	85.	(b)	112.	(b)	139.	(b)
5.	(c)	32.	(c)	59.	(d)	86.	(a)	113.	(c)	140.	(c)
6.	(d)	33.	(d)	60.	(d)	87.	(b)	114.	(b)	141.	(b)
7.	(a)	34.	(d)	61.	(a)	88.	(b)	115.	(d)	142.	(d)
8.	(d)	35.	(d)	62.	(c)	89.	(a)	116.	(d)	143.	(d)
9.	(c)	36.	(d)	63.	(c)	90.	(a)	117.	(d)	144.	(b)
10.	(b)	37.	(d)	64.	(c)	91.	(b)	118.	(b)	145.	(a)
11.	(d)	38.	(a)	65.	(b)	92.	(c)	119.	(b)	146.	(d)
12.	(b)	39.	(d)	66.	(b)	93.	(b)	120.	(d)	147.	(c)
13.	(c)	40.	(a)	67.	(d)	94.	(a)	121.	(c)		
14.	(b)	41.	(c)	68.	(c)	95.	(b)	122.	(d)		
15.	(c)	42.	(a)	69.	(d)	96.	(d)	123.	(c)		
16.	(d)	43.	(b)	70.	(c)	97.	(b)	124.	(d)		
17.	(?)	44.	(c)	71.	(c)	98.	(a)	125.	(c)		
18.	(c)	45.	(b)	72.	(d)	99.	(b)	126.	(d)		
19.	(a)	46.	(c)	73.	(d)	100.	(a)	127.	(a)		
20.	(d)	47.	(b)	74.	(d)	101.	(b)	128.	(d)		
21.	(d)	48.	(c)	75.	(b)	102.	(c)	129.	(d)		
22.	(d)	49.	(d)	76.	(a)	103.	(b)	130.	(c)		
23.	(b)	50.	(c)	77.	(c)	104.	(a)	131.	(c)		
24.	(c)	51.	(c)	78.	(c)	105.	(d)	132.	(b)		
25.	(b)	52.	(d)	79.	(d)	106.	(d)	133.	(c)		
26.	(d)	53.	(a)	80.	(a)	107.	(c)	134.	(a)		
27.	(b)	54.	(a)	81.	(c)	108.	(c)	135.	(c)		

EXERCISE 3

1.	(d)	13.	(a)	25.	(d)	37.	(a)	49.	(d)
2.	(c)	14.	(a)	26.	(d)	38.	(b)	50.	(c)
3.	(b)	15.	(d)	27.	(b)	39.	(a)		
4.	(d)	16.	(d)	28.	(b)	40.	(a)		
5.	(a)	17.	(a)	29.	(a)	41.	(c)		
6.	(b)	18.	(d)	30.	(a)	42.	(c)		
7.	(b)	19.	(d)	31.	(b)	43.	(c)		
8.	(b)	20.	(b)	32.	(b)	44.	(a)		
9.	(b)	21.	(d)	33.	(b)	45.	(b)		
10.	(b)	22.	(b)	34.	(d)	46.	(b)		
11.	(d)	23.	(a)	35.	(b)	47.	(c)		
12.	(d)	24.	(c)	36.	(a)	48.	(d)		